WAX ART

WAX ART

HAZEL MARSH

First published 2001 by
Guild of Master Craftsman Publications Ltd
Castle Place, 166 High Street,
Lewes, East Sussex BN7 1XU

Photographs by Chris Skarbon
with the exception of pages 1-3, courtesy of Ancient Art & Architecture Collection Ltd
Illustrations by John Yates

ISBN 1 86108 228 2

A catalogue record for this book is available from the British Library.

Editor: David Arscott
Book design: Danny McBride
Cover design: Joyce Chester

Set in Stone Serif, Humanist and Eras

Colour origination by Viscan Graphics (Singapore)
Printed and bound by Kyodo Printing (Singapore)

CONTENTS

Dedication:

*My gratitude and thanks to Steve,
Richard and Gemma for all their support
and encouragement*

ENCAUSTIC: decorated by any process involving burning in colours, esp. by inlaying coloured clays and baking or by fusing wax colours to the surface. From Greek enkaustikos, from enkaiein, to burn in.

Collins English Dictionary

Wax painting, or – to use its grander title – encaustic art, is a wonderfully simple decorating technique, which gives great results in minutes. Unlike many crafts, it really is as easy as it looks: there are just a few basic techniques to master before you start to produce your own quite spectacular results. The first time I saw someone demonstrating encaustic art at a craft fair I was completely bowled over, and I couldn't wait to get the basic equipment and have a go myself. That was several years ago, and now, when I am demonstrating myself, I see that same reaction in the people watching me.

Encaustic painting encourages fantasy and abstract images and the use of vivid colours, but don't be afraid to follow through themes which appeal to you – traditional or modern, muted or bold – and to use wax effects in combination with other decorating techniques, too. I'm sure you'll be delighted with what you can make. This really is a craft that anyone can take up, although you should always make sure that young children are supervised. If you enjoy surfing on-line, you'll find there's lots on encaustic art on the Internet: the interest is really growing.

Wax tomb portrait of a young man, Fayun 3rd century AD.

A LITTLE HISTORY

Wax painting isn't as modern as it may appear. In fact, the mummy portraits of Roman Egypt are the earliest examples of encaustic painting known to us – the oldest of them dating from AD 30–40, the latest from about AD 300. Having been preserved by an unusually dry climate, these wonderful pieces of art can be seen in museums all over the world.

The original encaustic techniques, together with the style of these surviving artefacts, seem to derive from the world of ancient Greece in the fourth century before Christ, while their survival owes everything to the Egyptians' profound belief in an afterlife. Expecting both spiritual and physical survival, and hoping eventually to be translated to the kingdom of Osiris, the god of the dead, the Egyptians made elaborate preparations for the journey from their earthly existence to the world beyond. These beliefs explain mummification and the inclusion in their tombs of food offerings and other objects.

Just as magic spells were placed in with the dead to ensure that their provisions would be replenished, these ancient people also believed that two- and three-dimensional images could usefully take the place of real things. In case the deceased body did not survive the journey to the afterlife they would furnish the grave with a substitute, such as a statue or a coffin shaped in human form. For the same reason masks and portraits were placed on or alongside the mummified body. The images accompanying the deceased were not supposed to be authentic likenesses, but rather their idealized, immortal images in the afterlife.

Our modern scientific testing suggests that several types of encaustic techniques were used in the ancient world, and that the painters of the mummy portraits were as individual in their approach as the artists of today. Different effects were achieved by using hot and cold wax, by treating the painting surface with materials such as glue and by using different tools (sometimes heated and sometimes cold) to apply the wax.

ENCAUSTIC ART TODAY

It is only in recent times that new techniques have stimulated a revival of interest in the subject. In 1986 Michael Bossom's wife bought him a work in wax and oil pastel by the French Canadian Jean-Marie Giraud, and this inspired him to experiment with the form, to develop many of the tools and much of the equipment now available and to write two books on the subject.

Those of us working in wax art today therefore owe Michael a debt of gratitude, however much we have developed some of our own ideas from his early promptings: indeed, his legacy will in part be the work of all those who have followed his example. In these pages you will find techniques such as waxing-over images and fabric printing of which he is the acknowledged master, and I also include the creation of texture in wax, printing with leaves and feathers and framing ideas, together with suggestions for home-made tools to create fantasy pictures.

To begin with, you'll probably want to make greetings cards or other simple projects using paper. There are so many possibilities with transferring melted wax, however, that I guarantee that you won't want to stop there.

It is worth reading the early sections to familiarize yourself with the basic principles of painting with an iron and wax blocks, but I hope that you will then want to try out the projects and be encouraged to develop different ideas for yourself. I've provided lots of 'hot tips' to help you achieve certain effects, and to show how the basic ideas can be elevated to a higher art form as your skills and confidence develop.

Ushabti figure of Tutankhamun.

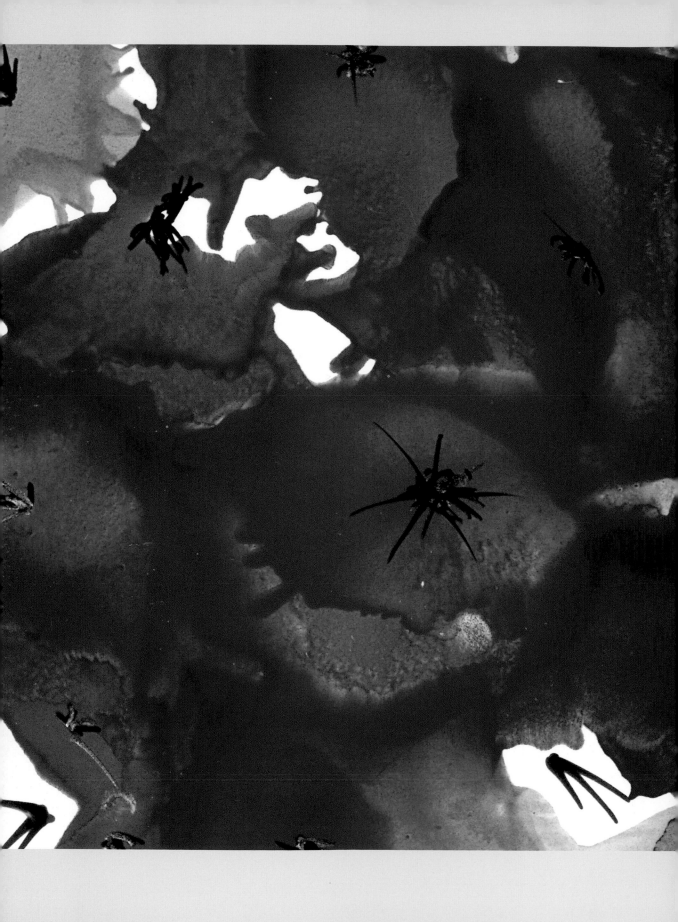

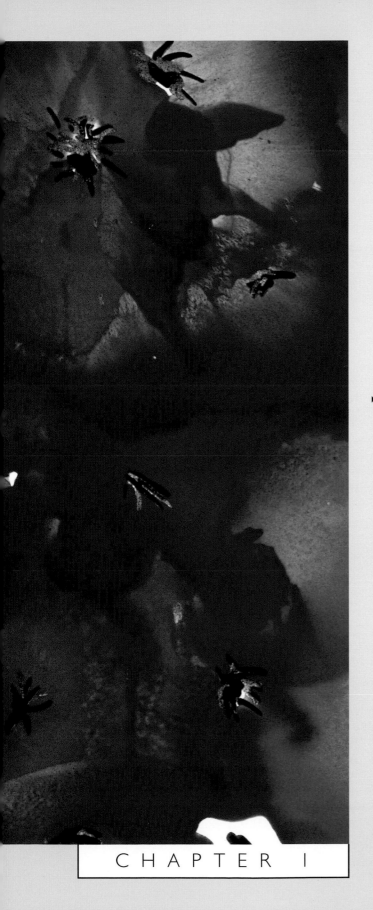

TOOLS, EQUIPMENT AND MATERIALS

CHAPTER I

BASIC TOOLS AND EQUIPMENT

Electric iron

The ideal iron to use is one that has been specifically developed for encaustic painting, with a good thermostatic control that can maintain a constant low heat. These irons, as we shall see later, can also be used as heated palettes.

A small travel iron performs reasonably well, but its thermostat is usually not as good. Large dry irons do work, but they are extremely cumbersome to use and, once again, the thermostat is normally less satisfactory. Irons with metal bases are far better than those with coated bases.

HOT TIP
Don't use a steam iron. The holes will become blocked, and the results will be messy.

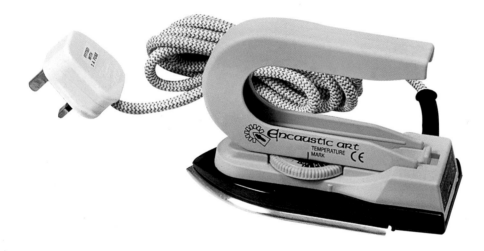

Above: The ideal iron will maintain a constant low heat.

Encaustic stylus

The encaustic stylus (facing page) is a tool especially developed by Michael Bossom. It is very similar to a soldering iron but has a much lower temperature. There is a range of tips to go with it: drawing tips, a small metal brush head and mini and micro iron tips. The stylus is a very useful piece of equipment which extends the range of techniques and effects that can be achieved. It will do all of the things which the iron tip can manage, but more easily and far more precisely. It is also easier to hold.

I have a wood-burning tool which is used for pyrography, but even this, on its lowest setting, is far too hot to use with wax.

Scribing tool

This is for scratching away wax to achieve various effects and for signing your artwork. In addition to the specially made scribing tool, I use a large sewing needle which has a much finer point.

Hot air paint stripper

For hot air blown effects. The normal setting is usually too hot, so buy one which also has a low setting. A hair dryer will work, but it needs to be a fairly powerful one.

Home-made tools.

As you progress you will hit upon ideas of your own for achieving various effects. I cover making your own tools on pages 36–39.

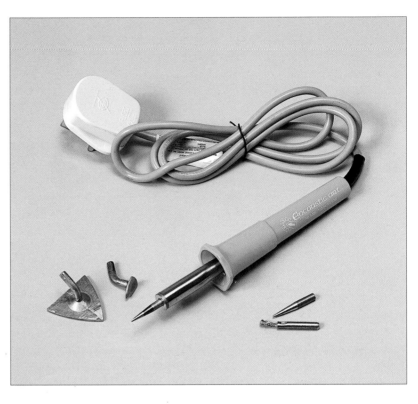

Above: An encaustic stylus gives you both precision and flexibility in your work.

Overalls

If you are a messy type of person (like me) it is essential to wear overalls or some similar protection, such as a large old T-shirt, that will cover your legs when you are sitting down. Molten wax drips very readily, and even one tiny drop can completely ruin an item of clothing. The wax itself will wash out in a fairly hot wash, but the coloured pigment is a different matter. The fact that it won't come out of fabrics easily, especially from natural materials such as cotton, is what allows us to use wax for printing on them in the first place.

Other equipment

In addition to this equipment you will need an old **sheet** or similar to cover your work surface and some **disposable paper** to go under your work. (You may be able to get hold of some used computer paper, in which case you can use the side which has no printing on it.) You will also need some **facial tissues** or **kitchen roll** for cleaning your iron, and some soft **tissues** or old **soft cloth** to polish up your finished work.

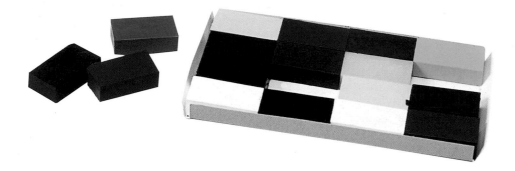

MATERIALS

Wax

There is a good range of specially formulated, encaustic, coloured wax blocks available which can be bought in sets or individually. I have tried wax crayons, but the results are extremely poor.

The various types and colours of wax blocks tend to have their own individual characteristics when being melted. Some, for example, are thicker than others. You will soon get the feel of them as you experiment with mixing colours together just as you would with paints.

Backings and painting card

The easiest backing to work on is a special encaustic art card. The list can, however, be as long as your imagination. I have tried many things, including wood, stone, tiles, candles and all sorts of different types of paper and card, both absorbent and non-absorbent. Fabric can have wax laid on it for use in collage, and it can be used to print on, too.

Work which is done on card can become cracked if the card is bent about too much, so to keep your works of art in really good condition it is always best to mount them on a more rigid backing.

Varnish

You should always buff your wax artwork with a pad of clean tissue or a soft cloth to give it a shine, but if it is something which will be handled quite often (a greetings card or a bookmark, for instance), you may want to give it a bit more protection. You can cover your wax masterpiece with a clear sticky backed film, but the best method is to varnish it, preferably with a quick-drying art quality acrylic spray varnish.

HOT TIP
Mix too many colours together and you will usually end up with a dirty brown splodge.

Other materials

For some of the projects in this book all sorts of other materials have been used, including **acrylic paints, ink, watercolour paints** and **felt tip pens**. For the chapter on adding extra texture to wax several odd materials have been used, such as **salt, sand,** old bits of **thread** and **wool, seeds, beads** and even **feathers**.

Transforming the pieces of wax art into finished articles such as framed pictures, cards, bookmarks etc. can call for all sorts of other equipment and materials, depending on what the project is. A **cutting mat** or **board, craft knife, pencil, steel ruler, set square, masking** and **double sided tape** are all things which will probably be needed to finish off most projects.

Some of the projects will need **greeting card blanks, bookmark blanks, mount card, picture frames, fabric, coloured card, felt pens, gold** and **silver pens** and **deckle cut craft scissors**. Don't be panicked by this long list, however, as there are many inexpensive ways of mounting and displaying wax art.

HOT TIP
Experiment with different backings: you may discover something really brilliant.

These colourful craft scissors allow cuts of various shapes to be made.

GETTING STARTED

ORGANIZING YOURSELF

First of all, get your work area organized. Protecting the surface you will be working on is very important, because molten wax has a tendency to drip and splash. Cover your work surface with an old cloth or sheet. It's not a bad idea to cover the floor around where you will be working, too. I learnt this lesson when I knocked my wax-loaded encaustic iron on to the floor and, of course, it landed wax-side down.

Place a pad of computer paper or a small pile of old newspapers where you will be sitting, with a sheet of clean paper on top. Do always keep a pile of clean paper to hand, because the paper positioned under the painting card will need to be changed fairly regularly. The beauty of a computer pad is that the dirty piece can just be torn off, revealing a new piece already in place.

Below: Ready to begin

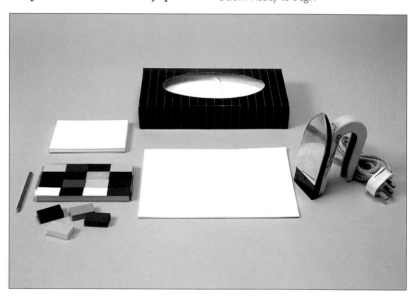

If you are right handed, position your iron at the front of your work surface to your right and a pad of tissues or torn off kitchen roll towards the back along with a box of tissues or a soft cloth ready for polishing.

On your left hand side lay out your wax blocks and, behind them, a pile of ready-cut painting card. Directly opposite you, towards the back, have this book open and ready. If you are left handed then just reverse all this.

PREPARING THE IRON

Below : Loading the iron.

At last, the exciting part! Plug your painting iron in, set the thermostat control to low and wait a couple of minutes for it to get warm.

Hold your iron upside down, with the base plate uppermost so that it is horizontal – not at a tilt. Choose a wax block and touch it onto the iron so that it starts to melt. Now gently rub it onto the iron: this is called loading the iron.

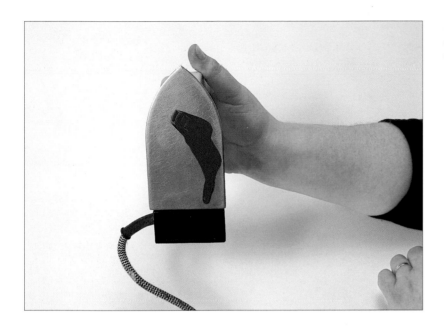

If the iron is too hot the wax will drip all over the place. Adjust the heat so that the wax runs down it very slowly.

CLEANING YOUR IRON

You will need to clean your iron after each application of wax colour. Simply wipe the iron over the pile of tissues or kitchen roll to clean the base plate. To get at any wax lurking in the crevice between the base plate and the top of the iron, fold some tissues so that you can wipe in there, too.

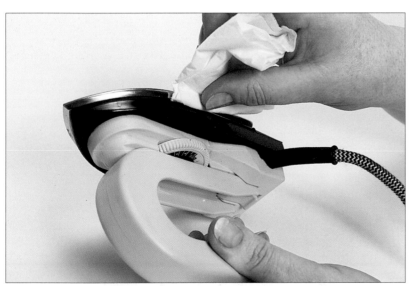

For a more thorough clean, melt some clear wax onto the iron and then give it a good wipe off with tissues.

IRON MANOEUVRING AND EFFECTS

Have a really good play around with each different technique. You will soon get the feel of it all and be surprised at some of the wonderful effects you achieve.

HOT TIP
Don't push down on the iron, but let it gently glide across the card.

Smoothing.

This is just like ironing clothes, but with a much lighter touch. Load up the iron with one or more colours. Several different effects can be achieved, depending upon the way the iron is loaded up and is smoothed across the card. Load the iron with lots of white and then just add a dab of two of other colours. Smooth the iron across the card with the tip pointing to the top of the card. The effect will change every time you smooth it across. Take a soft cloth or pad of tissue and give the wax on the painting card a gentle buff up.

The loaded iron. You can always add more wax if it looks a bit sparse, or you can choose to dab a small amount of extra colour on to the iron and smooth that across.

Take a new piece of card, load the iron with wax and then smooth it across the surface, moving the iron in a gentle up and down motion as you go along. Give the wax a gentle polish.

Mountains after the smoothing process.

Load the iron with two colours, and smooth the iron across the bottom half of the card point first. As you glide the iron along, move your hand very slightly up and down to produce a 'hilly' effect. This technique is the basis of landscape painting.

Load the iron with one colour of wax, adding a few dabs of other colours if you like. Start with the point of the iron in the centre of the card and then carefully smooth it to the outside, gently wiggling and wriggling the iron as you go.

Lifting and dabbing

Load the iron with one or more wax colours. Place the iron down onto the card and quickly lift it off again. This can be done on top of a ready-laid wax background or direct onto the plain card. It can be done with just the tip of the iron, just the sides or with the whole iron. The process can also be reversed by holding the iron and dabbing the card onto it.

HOT TIP
Don't forget to polish up your finished results and see what a difference it makes.

When using the edge of the iron, hold it at an angle of up to about 45° from the card.

Load some wax onto the iron just on the edge where it touches the card and do some more strokes, re-loading the iron as necessary.

Using the edge of the iron

This technique uses the edge of the iron at the point where the straight side starts to curve up to the point. On a ready prepared wax background imagine that the edge of your iron is an ice skate and glide it up and down on the card. Try taking the iron off the card at the end of each stroke, then (for a completely different effect) lowering the angle of the iron and zigzagging it across the card.

Drawing with the iron tip

In order to draw with the tip, start with a ready-done wax background. Hold your iron in whichever position is most comfortable for you – I hold mine upside down.

First draw onto the wax with the tip of the iron.

Now touch the tip of the iron onto a wax block (almost as if dipping a pen into an ink pot) and make drawing marks on top of the wax on the card.

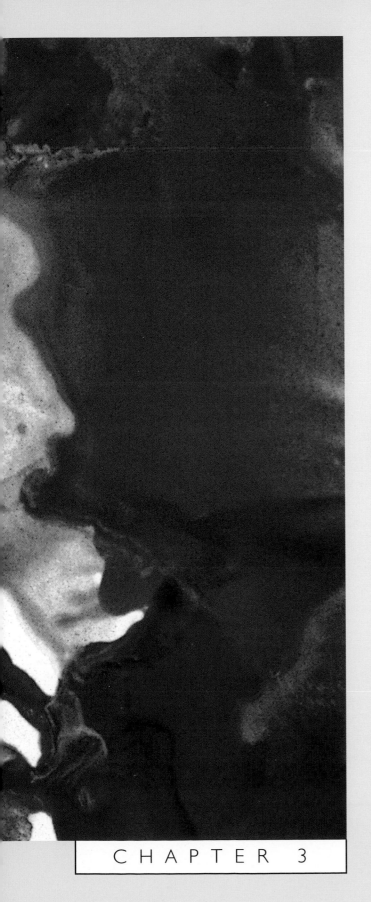

PAINTING
LANDSCAPES WITH
THE IRON

CHAPTER 3

HORIZONS AND FOREGROUNDS

There is no shortage of inspiration here. Just gaze around you the next time you are out in the countryside. Try to look beyond the 'beautiful view' and take in the amount of different colours, shades and shapes. Look in books, at postcards and at calendars: the list is seemingly endless. The colour of the sky is often reflected in the landscape, and there are areas of shadow and areas of light. Do you want your landscape to be bright and sunny or dark and menacing? Do you want to give the impression of snow-capped mountains? Keep all these things in mind as you come to paint your landscapes.

To get started, load up your iron with colour – roughly the top left hand quarter of it. Let's start with green for a natural look, and then introduce a thin line of colour from the brown/orange range down the edge of the iron on top of the green.

Smooth the iron across the card from right to left either straight across for a flat horizon or a gentle fluid up-and-down movement for hills. Take the iron right off the edge so that you get a continuous flowing line, and don't be tempted to lift the iron while it is on the card. Now bring the iron back across the card from right to left, further down than the last stroke but overlapping it slightly.

Continue zigzagging down the card in this manner to the bottom, loading up with more wax if needed. To achieve more rocky or mountainous horizons, load up just the top inch or so of the tip of the iron. Add a little splodge of another colour, either in the middle of your first colour or just round the top edge of the tip. The colours you use will depend upon what you are trying to achieve: for snow-topped mountains try using grey with white around the tip edge.

HOT TIP
Keep trying until you achieve something you like. I still sometimes make a hideous mess.

The iron loaded for the beginning of the picture.

The part-painted hilly landscape, smoothed across.

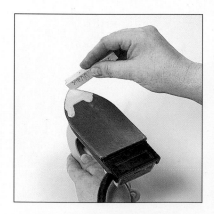

Iron tip loaded up with grey and white for snow.

This time instead of smoothing across the card tip first, work from left to right with the tip pointing towards the top of the card. Start midway down the card and lift the heel of the iron up slightly so that just the tip of the iron (with the colour on it) is touching the card. Gently smooth across the card, making up and down movements as you go.

If you want to create very spiky mountains, load the wax onto the iron on the righthand side of the plate (as you look down on it with the iron upside down) just around the area where the iron starts to curve.

With the waxed part of the iron touching the card and the iron at a slight angle, again smooth across the card, making up-and-down movements as you go.

Load the side of the iron.

The mountains begin to form . . .

. . . and are given a spiky effect.

Now have a go at making some horizons with a mixture of effects, rolling hills and an outcrop of craggy mountains.

HOT TIP
Try to relax while you are painting, because it helps to keep your movements more fluid.

19

SKY

With landscapes you can just leave the top part of your picture blank, letting the white card show, or you can add some colour to it, giving depth and interest.

There are basically two ways to make a coloured sky: first, crayoning and rubbing, which tends to produce a fairly soft, calm sky; and secondly, smoothing with the iron, which can achieve really dramatic effects.

Crayoning and rubbing

It is best to add this type of sky to a ready-painted foreground. Choose the colours that you want to use, making sure that the wax blocks are clean on the end you are going to 'crayon' with. Remember that real skies can be the most incredible colours, so it's worth experimenting on some spare card in order to get the exact effect you are looking for. It is often good to leave a small section in the middle blank: this helps to give depth to the picture.

Once you have settled on the colours, gently rub the wax blocks on the sky area of your picture as if crayoning.

Finally blend the colours by rubbing reasonably firmly with your finger.

HOT TIP
Always make sure that your rubbing finger is clean.

Smoothing with the iron

With this method the sky must be painted before the landscape horizon and foreground. Again, your sky can be whatever colour you want it to be, but begin by loading your iron with lots of white and then introduce a streak of blue and a hint of pink.

By using different actions and movements with the iron amazing effects can be achieved, from a serene bright summer sky to a raging stormy one.

The very best way to discover how to achieve different effects is by trial and error. Experiment with colour combinations, with the way that you smooth the iron across the card and with the angle you have the iron as you are smoothing. Try smoothing over the sky a second and third time. Alternatively, you could add some more colour to the iron and go over the top of the wax already laid down. Try using clear wax as a base when loading up the iron, and then adding a few colours to this.

The iron loaded with blue and pink.

Below: Painted landscape pictures showing different coloured skies.

ADDING DETAIL – THE FOLIAGE EFFECT

By now you should have in front of you a card with or without a wax sky and a horizon. If there is not plenty of wax on the card right down to the bottom, smooth on a bit more in the same main colour you have used for the horizon.

We are now going to dab the iron onto the bottom part of the picture to create the effect of foliage. Dab the iron onto the waxed card and then lift it off: try doing this at different angles. You will notice that dabbing and lifting the iron in this way leaves marks where the edge of the iron has touched the card. Sometimes this will be exactly the effect you are after, but you can achieve a softer and more natural look by using a slightly different technique. Smooth some more wax over the dabbing you have just done. This time hold the card up, gripping it firmly between your thumb and a couple of fingers at the top. Now hold the iron in a horizontal position to the card and dab it on and off of the card, making sure that you don't allow the edge of the iron to touch the wax.

Extra colour can be added to the foliage effect. Choose two colours that will harmonize with your horizon and sky colours, put a squiggle of each on the iron and then dab it on to the foreground of your picture – again using the hand-held method.

Dabbing the iron onto the horizon.

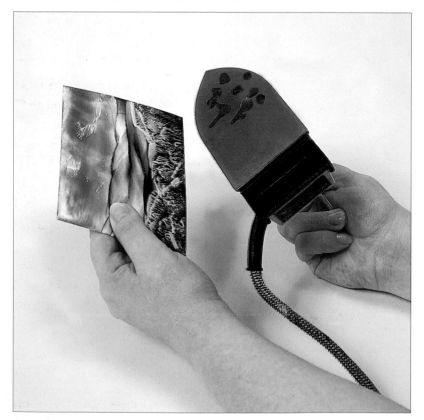

GRASSES AND REEDS

By using the edge of the iron like an ice skate going through the wax already on the card, put in a clump of grasses or reeds. Make some of the strokes longer than others, with some going off at a slight angle. Add just a touch of colour to the side of the iron, such as brown for reeds, and repeat the strokes. Do some with extra colour and some without – see what you like best.

WATER

There are two ways to produce a water effect. The first is to wipe away wax with a small pad of tissue while the wax is still warm. After putting the foliage effect in to your picture, wipe across parallel to the top of the card, leaving a small amount of the foliage above the water.

HOT TIP
Don't wipe over the card too many times or the effect will be lost.

The second way to add water to your landscapes is with wax. Remember that water is reflective, and so the colours in the sky will show in the water: if there are towering mountains on the horizon they may well be casting a shadow over the water, as will trees and foliage. There may be patches of light and patches of dark dancing around on the surface, too. The wonderful thing here is that these are just the sort of effects that wax naturally produces.

Lakes, ponds and sea

Start off with a card that has a ready-painted sky and a horizon just above the midway point. Carry out about ½inch (13mm) of hand-held dabbing at the base of the horizon to create the effect of foliage at the far side of the water. Load up your iron as you would for a sky. Using the same colours that appear in this particular sky, smooth the iron across the lower part of the card, just very slightly overlapping the bottom of the foliage band. This slight overlapping mixes in some of the darker colour and gives the effect of shadow. You may need to smooth over the water area again to get just the right look.

HOT TIP
The wax on the card can be re-heated by holding the iron upside down and then just touching the back of the card onto the iron.

Once you have your water in place you may wish to consider doing a bit more hand dabbing with the foliage colours around the bottom of the water and perhaps up the side as well, creating a lake or pond.

Streams

Fold a tissue into a small pad and then either roll it up and twist it to form a point, or twist a good thick layer of tissue around the end of the scribing tool or a pencil. With the card flat on the work surface, and while the wax is still warm, rub out colour with the tissue. Starting midway down your foreground, curve it round a bit, as if the stream is meandering through your picture, making it wider and wider as it comes down to the bottom.

Rubbing off wax while it is still warm.

Try not to use too much pressure when wiping across with fairly quick strokes.

Load some clear wax on to the iron and smooth this across the water, or alternatively create the water from scratch by loading clear wax onto the iron and adding just a touch of the other colours from the sky.

PATHS, TRACKS AND ROADS

Use the same basic method as for streams but scratch away the cold wax with the scribe tool or anything else that will do the job. Start in the distance and work to the front, curving the path round and making it wider and wider as it comes to the front of your picture. If you have a hilly horizon and foreground you can start far off in the distance with just the hint of a path. Make it disappear for a while and later emerge slightly larger from behind another hill – you'll find that this will give real depth to the picture.

FENCES AND POSTS

Load the tip of the iron with fence-coloured wax and put a small spot onto the card. Drag the tip down to create a fence post and then add others, making them smaller and with less space between them as they disappear into the distance.

It is possible to draw trees using the tip of the iron, but you would need to have a fair bit of artistic flare to make them look realistic. My attempts always seem to look a little childish, so I tend to use the heated stylus tool instead.

BIRDS

Using the very tip of the iron, dip into a brown colour and then make two or three tiny dots in the sky. (The size of the dots will determine how near or far away the birds appear to be.) Clean the tip of the iron, touch it back on to one of the dots and flick it first one way and then the other making a fairly wide open V shape.

DRAGONFLIES

Basically the same technique as for birds, but a bit more of a fiddle. This time use dragonfly colours – green, blue and maybe a touch of one of the metallic waxes. Place a small dot so that it will look as if the dragonfly is hovering over the water or in among the reeds and grasses. Then, with a clean iron tip, lightly flick the wax from the dot twice on one side and twice on the other, making a very open flat V shape with the double pair of wings. Finally, with a tiny amount of a slightly stronger colour, dot just above the centre of the wings, clean the tip and flick that dot down, curving it a little as you go.

FLOWERS

Flowers in a landscape are very easily created by simply touching the tip of the iron onto whichever colour wax you want and then making varying sized dots and tiny daubs on the foliage areas. I think the best effect is achieved by doing small clumps and swathes of them. (We look at more advanced techniques with flowers on pages 30–33.)

HOT TIP
Don't forget to polish your finished pictures by buffing gently with a pad of clean tissue or soft cloth.

USING HOT AIR FOR BLOWN EFFECTS

Some very interesting effects can be achieved by introducing hot air to wax. A good quality, fairly powerful, hair dryer will normally do the trick, although a hot air paint stripper works better. When I first had a go at this, to be honest, the idea of using a paint stripper scared me to death, but with my husband's encouragement and close supervision I summoned up all my courage and had a go.

Actually it wasn't as scary as I had thought it would be. My advice is never to use it above its very lowest setting and to make sure that you keep your fingers out of the way.

The other thing to remember is to use the paint stripper in short bouts only, letting it cool right down before using it again. Don't keep it directed in one place for too long, because if it gets too hot for the job, the card will start to bubble and pucker.

Basically what happens is that the hot air melts the wax and then distributes it across the card in whichever direction the air flow is going. A good thing about this technique is that no marks are left by the iron or any other tools.

At this point you may well be saying to yourself 'Oh, dear' – but don't despair! By adding just a few small details this messy looking collection of splodges will be transformed into a wonderful 'impressionist' work of art. Using the tip of the iron (or the stylus, if you have one) start adding small black or dark-coloured lines and dots in the centre of each flower head. The difference will immediately be amazing. Go on to add foliage and leaves, first using the edge of the iron like a skating blade and then the iron tip to put in extra feathery detail to the leaves. A stylus, of course, makes putting in detail a little bit more precise.

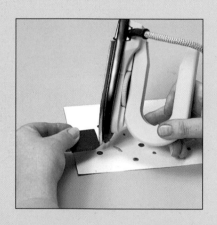

First melt some 15 to 20 small blobs of wax on to your painting card by touching the iron tip on a wax block and letting a small amount drip onto the card. To begin with, use two or three different colours. Above all, be bold: experiment by putting different combinations of colours together.

Once all your little blobs are in place, turn your hot air stripper on to the very lowest setting and hold it fairly close to the wax – approximately 2–2½in (5–7cm) – directly over the top of each blob in turn.

As soon as the blob starts to melt, move the hot air around slightly so that the flow goes in different directions: this takes a little bit of playing with until you get the feel of it. The aim is to turn the little blobs into abstract-shaped 'splodges', each one slightly intermingling with the ones around it.

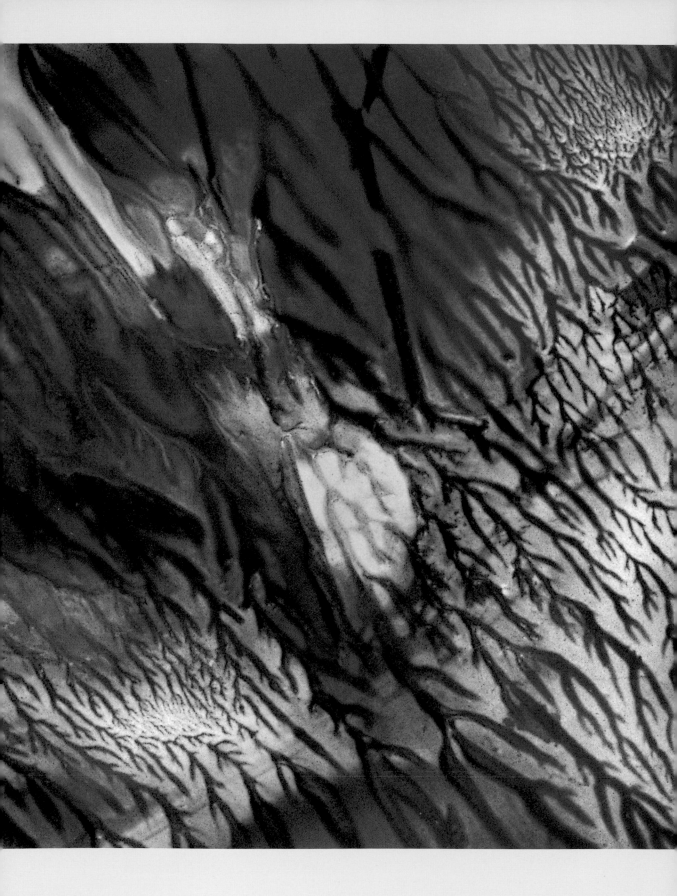

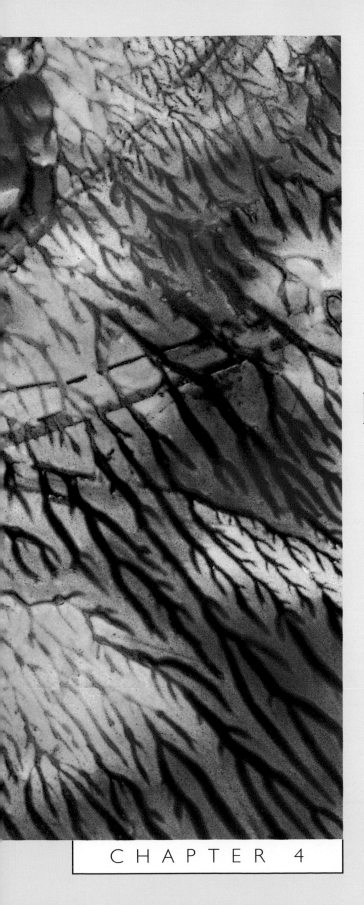

Painting Pictures with the Iron

FLOWERS

Encaustic painting is more about effects and impressions than ending up with a meticulously accurate reproduction of real life, although some kinds of flowers do end up looking surprisingly like the real thing. Poppies and corn are quite good, as are daffodils, foxgloves and cornflowers.

Foxgloves.

Above: Framed picture of cornflowers.

Others, however, are almost impossible to get right. (A rose in full bloom with multi-layered petals is one of them.) Personally I'm not at all bothered whether a wax-painted flower looks like a particular species or not: as long as it resembles a flower of some sort and is pretty, that's really all that matters. If you look around you at designs for other things like wallpaper and fabric, you will see that this is often the case.

Left: Daffodils.

Make-believe flowers (left) and framed picture of poppies and corn (far left).

The background for a flower picture can either be left as blank card, or you can paint a wax background. On the whole it is probably better to stick to just one colour, perhaps mixed with white or clear. Load the iron and smooth the wax across the card, filling the whole of it.

HOT TIP
Don't go too mad with the background design or it will detract from your main subject, the flowers.

The background can be left as it is, or you can, instead, use the dabbing and lifting method all over the card in a random pattern.

Try dabbing and lifting the iron on and off of the card, placing the point of the iron in the centre then working your way around the whole card.

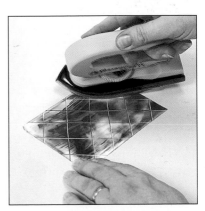

To add something extra, try drawing a latticework over the top of the card by using the iron on its edge like an ice skate.

If you are doing a picture of a group of flowers it is probably best to paint in some leaves and greenery first. Do this by loading some green wax on to the side edge of the iron and then using the iron like an ice skate, as we have done before.

Flowers do certainly need a little bit of practice. To start with, take a blank card and, holding your iron the normal way up, touch the side of the tip onto a block of wax. How much of the iron gets wax on it depends on how big you want your flower to be.

If you want a flower with ½inch (13mm) petals then touch just the first ½inch from the tip down the left side of the iron on to the wax.	To get the effect of a multi-layered bloom, go round the flower again doing smaller petals just in from the last ones.	A mixture of coloured blobs can be highly effective.

Now touch the waxed part of the iron on to the card with the iron at a slight angle, and gently move the very tip of the iron around so that you spread the wax out into a petal shape. Next move the card round, dip the iron on the wax again and do another petal shape on the card next to the last one, curving it down a little. Continue to do this, turning the card as you go until you end up with a circle of petals. It doesn't matter if your petal circle looks rather flat or a bit of a funny shape, and it doesn't matter if some petals are bigger than others – in fact this often helps to make the flowers look more realistic.

Once you have achieved a 'circle' of petals, dip the iron tip onto a contrasting coloured wax (black often works well) and then put a blob on the middle of the flower to make the centre. Then, using the very tip of the iron, tease out some of the wax from the blob. Adding some tiny dots of the same colour just around the outside of the centre can look really good, and so can adding a few very small blobs of another colour to the centre, including some of the metallic colour waxes.

HOT TIP
Try holding your iron in different ways until you find a position you are comfortable with.

To produce flowers in other stages of openness we use the same basic method – for buds just smoothing the wax round a tiny amount. Another way of getting a flower effect is by putting a small blob of wax on to the card and then, with the tip of the iron, flicking out from the blob all the way around until you have a daisy-type flower.

When we look at real flowers the heads are facing all sorts of different ways and we see them at many different angles. We can achieve this effect by varying the length and quantity of wax spread around in a petal shape, the amount of wax we load on the iron and the area of iron we place on the card.

For corn, paint pairs of very tight petals in a V shape one on top the other, and then with a clean iron tip – and starting at the base – draw quick, flicking lines through each petal shape. Foxglove-type flowers are created in a similar fashion, but the other way up.

HOT TIP
The key word again is Experiment.

Depth can be added by adding touches of lighter and darker wax to create light and shadow on the plants. To add stems and leaves to individual flowers, first dip the iron tip on a green wax block and dot a small blob in the appropriate place on the flower. Next, using the tip of the iron, spread some of the green wax up each side of the base of the petals or the bud with a flicking motion, then (again with a clean iron tip) dot back on to the blob and quickly flick down to make the stem.

HOT TIP
Polish up your finished pictures by lightly buffing with a soft cloth or a pad of clean tissue.

FANTASY

Painting fantasy pictures with wax is great fun, because you can really let your imagination run wild and you don't have to conform to any pre-set ideas about which colour anything should be.

Mostly the methods are very similar to those used for landscape painting, plus a few extra ones to achieve effects such as planets or castles with lighted windows and winding steps. We can add bats or dragons in the way that we added birds, but with black wax instead.

Above and left: Once you master the basics you can produce pictures like these in just a few minutes.

Castles

Start off by painting a sky and a horizon, and then decide where the castle is going to go – preferably in a fairly central position. Touch the iron on to a wax block, choosing the same sort of colour as the background, and then, using the very tip and just the edge of the tip, start to work the colour from the iron into the background colour. Draw the wax up to achieve a vertical block of straight lines parallel to the edge of the card. Continue to take up more wax and work upwards, varying the length of the lines so that you achieve a castle shape.

Once you are happy with your castle, do a little bit of hand-held dabbing around the base of it to help blend it into the background. You could have another castle in the picture: to make it look further away, place it on a hill that stands back in the picture and make it much smaller.

Now scratch away a little of the wax here and there to make some windows. To give a really three-dimensional effect, scratch away a series of parallel horizontal lines to look like steps. Dotting sets of these steps around gives a wonderful illusion of dark corners and interesting winding passageways.

HOT TIP
Remember that metal conducts heat and will burn you if touched.

Creating a castle in the landscape.

Scratching the steps of the castle.

Planets and moons

Planets are basically circles filled in with wax, using the end of the iron. Perfect circles look far better, so freehand is not ideal. One solution is to place a penny or something similar on the sky area of your picture and carefully scratch round it with a sewing needle. I create planets using a simple gadget that my husband made for me (see page 39). Using a hacksaw, he cut a small piece of copper pipe about 1in (3cm) long (the type that plumbers use) and smoothed off the cut edge of pipe, using a very fine file and some wire wool. He then made a handle by tapering a piece of wooden dowel at one end and wedging it into the pipe.

HOT TIP
Take care not to let the nail head slide about on the wax.

To make a perfect circle for a planet just hold the pipe on to the iron, using the wooden handle, so that the metal heats up.

Place it on the sky area, being careful not to let it slide about, then twist it around a fraction and lift it off.

The outline can now be filled in, using the tip of the iron.

Above: Fantasy scene with nail head planets and moons.

I found another very easy way of doing planets was to use the round head of a nail. I raided my husband's workshop and found myself an assortment of nails with various sized heads, making sure I picked only those with nice smooth tops. I hammered the nails part way into small blocks of wood until they were firmly held – you could, as an equally effective alternative, push the nails into old wine bottle corks.

By grasping the wooden block I could then safely hold the nail head against the iron to heat up. Once this had been done, I dabbed the circular head on a block of wax and immediately placed it on the sky area of my picture, giving it a gentle twist before lifting off.

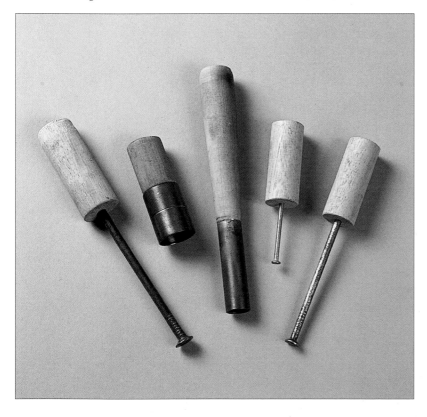

Left: The author's home-made moon and planet kit comprises nails, copper pipe and oddments of wood.

Another way of making a very effective background for a fantasy picture is by loading up your iron with stripes of colour going across it and then smoothing it over the card, lifting the leading edge of the iron as you go. Once you have achieved a pretty dramatic effect, turn the card to the portrait position with the stripes of colour going top to bottom, and then put in your horizon, foreground and so on. If you have a fairly dark sky, try scratching away a tiny bit of wax to look like a distant sparkling star, and scratch a scattering of minute pin-prick dots around to give the effect of a night sky. Polish up your finished picture to a lovely shine.

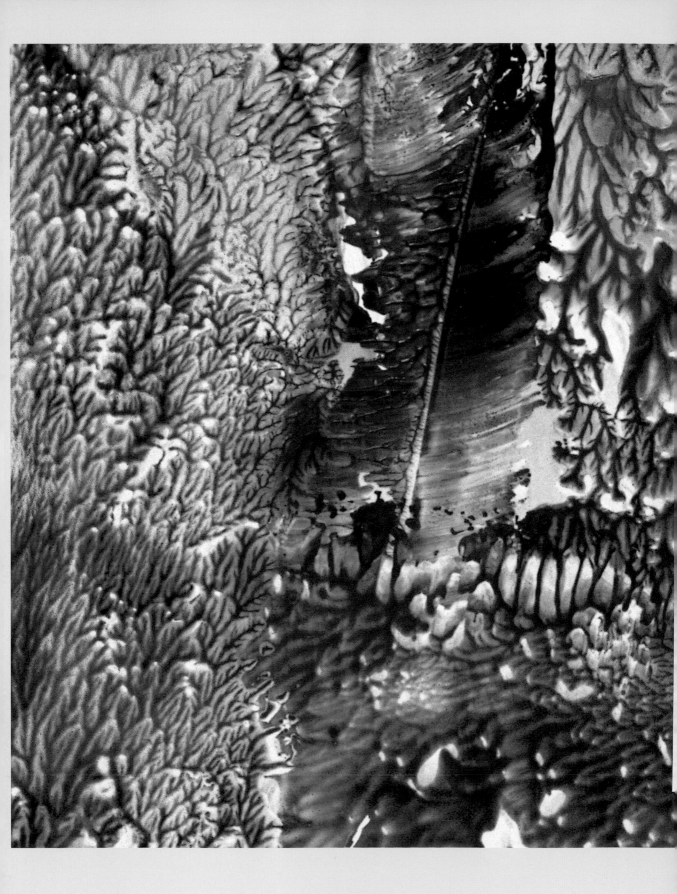

Wax Painting on Other Backgrounds

All the way through this book we have done most of our wax painting on special shiny encaustic art card. This is certainly the easiest and most obvious surface to work on, but there are many others, too. I have always experimented, and I sometimes catch myself eyeing up objects when I'm out and about, thinking 'I just wonder . . .?'

To start with, let's think about surfaces which have similar qualities to the encaustic card – a shiny, smooth surface on which wax can be moved around using the iron.

CERAMIC WALL TILES

I talk about using ceramic wall tiles in the chapter on fabric printing (page 85). The advantage of painting onto tiles as opposed to card is that they are not flexible, and the wax is therefore less likely to get cracked – something that it might do on a card that was inadvertently bent about.

Here is a simple project using a 6in (15cm) square ceramic tile which you can hang on your kitchen wall. After doing your wax painting on the tile you will need to protect it by giving it several coats of varnish, either sprayed or applied by brush (use an art quality acrylic varnish).

To frame the tile, you will need:

1 piece of ¼ or ⅜in (6mm or 9mm) plywood 7½in (19cm) square

2 lengths of ¾ x ⁵⁄₁₆in (2cm x 8mm) prepared soft wood 7½in (19cm) long

2 two lengths of ¾ x⁵⁄₁₆in (2cm x 8mm) prepared soft wood 6 in (15cm) long.

(You can make the frame wider or narrower should you wish: simply recalculate the sizes needed.)

For the backing you will need:

1 piece of plywood 6in (15cm) square plus twice the width of the softwood frame.

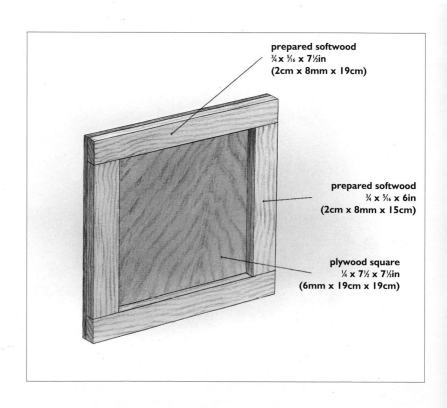

prepared softwood
¾ x ⁵⁄₁₆ x 7½in
(2cm x 8mm x 19cm)

prepared softwood
¾ x ⁵⁄₁₆ x 6in
(2cm x 8mm x 15cm)

plywood square
¼ x 7½ x 7½in
(6mm x 19cm x 19cm)

First cut two pieces of softwood framing which are the same length as the plywood and two pieces the same length as the tile. Attach the frame pieces to the plywood backing using wood glue, and then hammer a few panel pins through the back of the plywood.

Once the glue is set, give the frame a quick sand down with fine sandpaper, and then give the softwood frame pieces and the back of the plywood a coat of acrylic varnish. When the varnish is dry give the whole frame another quick sand and another coat of varnish, but do not varnish the plywood where the tile will go. It is probably best to leave the frame for at least several hours or overnight to dry thoroughly. Coat the back of your wax painted ceramic tile with tile adhesive and firmly position it in the frame.

SMOOTH PEBBLES

I didn't find it very easy to paint directly on to pebbles using the iron, so I had to devise another way of doing it. Experimenting, I found that if I heated up the pebbles themselves they held their heat for long enough to use the wax blocks directly on them. To heat a pebble, place it in a microwave oven on the high setting for about 1–1½ minutes or in a normal oven 200°C/400°F/ Gas mark 6 for up to 5 minutes, but no longer.

Once you have a nice thick coating of wax on the pebble, start adding other colours – either by using the wax block directly, gently smoothing wax on with the tip of the iron, or by melting the wax with the iron tip and allowing it to drip onto the pebble. With the pebble still hot, and the wax coating still in a molten state, any new wax that is introduced tends to intermingle, producing rather interesting effects.

WARNING

Don't go away forgetting that you have pebbles heating in your oven. I shall never forget making a driftwood fire with a group of friends on a shingle beach. Red hot pebbles started to shoot out of it in all directions, putting paid to any hope of cooking our sausages. It was also very frightening.

HOT TIP
When working with hot pebbles, place them on a thick pad of folded rags and always wear oven gloves.

Remember that pebbles do hold heat for quite some time, so you will need to be a bit patient here. It is safest to leave your painted pebble to cool down for several hours before you attempt to polish it up with tissue or a soft cloth. After this it can be varnished.

The sort of painting that can be done with this technique is pretty abstract and has a rather naïve charm to it. Personally I think that pebbles painted in this way make really attractive, very colourful paper weights.

WOOD

Bare wood tends to be too porous, soaking the wax into its fibres and so making it impossible to move the wax around as you would when painting onto encaustic card. Overcome this by applying several coats of varnish first, by priming the surface to be painted with acrylic paint or by sealing the surface with a watered down solution of PVA glue.

HOT TIP
Do make sure that whatever you use as a sealant is completely dry before attempting to paint on the wax.

COLOURED GLOSSY CARD

White and sparkly white wax painted on black or dark-coloured card can create a stunning picture which gives an effective impression of snow and ice.

I have found that mixing in some clear or clear sparkly wax with the other colours produces pleasing results with a translucent quality.

Glossy coated coloured card is also really good for printing leaves and feathers.

Right: Using coloured card as a background gives striking results.

Left: Fantasy pictures painted on glossy coloured card can have a haunting, surreal quality.

Right: Imaginary scenes allow you to let your hair down with garish colour combinations.

Left: Wax effects lend themselves to dream (or nightmare) landscapes.

Right: Leaf prints are among the easiest things to do.

Above: This feather print is simple but highly effective.

CANDLES

It's very easy to turn a plain candle into a rather exotic looking one. Assemble the iron in its hotplate mode (see page 68) and load it up with a nice swirled mixture of colours. It's always nice to add a bit of metallic colour. Next – taking care not to burn your fingers – roll the candle across the surface of the hotplate. What happens is that the surface of the candle melts a little and picks up (and blends with it) the coloured wax from the iron.

Re-load the iron as many times as you need to, and continue to work your way down the candle, a section at a time, until the whole of it is covered.

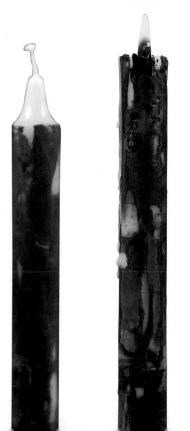

Left: A plain candle is transformed into something special.

ABSORBENT PAPER, CARD AND FABRIC

Some lovely effects can be achieved by applying wax to absorbent materials. Do remember that, because the fibres absorb the wax pigment so that it becomes ingrained into the material, it is not possible to move the wax around as we would for normal wax painting on encaustic card. This means that no changes can be made.

Apart from many types of fabric, there are all sorts of different papers and cards to try. Some, including an abundance of hand-made papers, have wonderful textures. Try watercolour paper and even blotting paper. Absorbent materials are excellent for printing leaves and feathers on, because in this case we don't want to move the wax around.

COLLAGE AND EMBROIDERY

This in another area in which we can use absorbent materials impregnated with wax.

The background of this collage is a length of canvas to which I applied some blue and copper-coloured wax.

Also used in this piece of work is some hessian with copper-coloured wax on it and some hand-made paper with a mixture of blue, white and copper wax. A small piece of encaustic card has been added to the collage, after being coated with burgundy and copper-coloured wax and textured with seed beads. There are also a few strands of wax-covered wool which have been pulled off an encaustic card which had wool added to it as a texture. (See pages 68-69.)

The hessian was very roughly sewn on to the dark blue background with machine embroidery thread, using a sewing machine's zigzag stitch.

Everything else was sewn on by hand, in a deliberately very haphazard way, using copper-coloured embroidery thread.

Making the copper coils is a very simple process: different thicknesses of copper wire can be stripped out from a length of old electrical wire and wound round and round something like a sewing needle until they reach the required size. The needle is then pulled out from the coil.

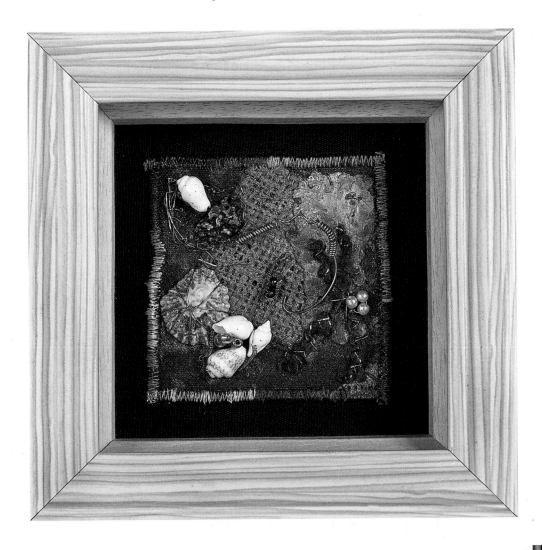

INDIRECT WAX PAINTING

This is a technique which gives some lovely soft effects and is a lot of fun to do as well. So far we have always loaded wax on to the iron and then painted directly on to the card. With indirect wax painting, however, we first load coloured wax from the iron on to a soft tissue or piece of cloth, and we then use this to put colour and shapes on our painting card.

To start, lay out an opened-up tissue on top of the under paper, then melt some wax colour (blue, for example) onto the iron. Wipe this on to a small part of the tissue. Repeat this with a second colour (green, perhaps) and then again with a third colour, such as orange/brown.

Place the loaded tissue onto a new piece of painting card, wax-side down, then – keeping the back of the iron slightly raised – put the tip on the tissue. Using small and fairly abrupt movements, push down on the tissue so that the colour transfers to the card. This takes a little practice, but try using lots of different strokes in different directions.

Once you get the hang of it, it really is quite easy to make what looks like a pile of rocks. Next rub with your finger around the base of this pile to smear the wax so that it takes on the look of water. Grasses can be added as for a normal landscape picture, but this time through the wax-loaded tissue and using a little more pressure than normal. I know I'm always saying it, but please don't forget to polish up your finished pieces of artwork.

Make sure that you slightly overlap each colour as you work.

Keep looking under the tissue to see how things are developing.

HOT TIP
Try out lots of different combinations of colour and you may end up with some wonderfully surreal art.

WAXING OVER
IMAGES

CHAPTER 6

I am particularly fond of this technique, as the possibilities seem endless. The basics are simple: you use all sorts of different methods and materials in order to place pictures, images and words under a translucent wax finish. If you have access to a computer, clip art can be printed straight on to the encaustic painting card. Rubber stamping also works well, and you can trace shapes, pictures and words and then fill them in or go over them with ink, felt pen or acrylic paints. You can do the same with stencils, too, although if you are reasonably artistic you will probably prefer to draw or paint your own designs. Blown-ink pictures look spectacular, as do symmetrical printed ink-blob pictures, but my favourite is the use of calligraphy under the wax.

HOT TIP
Make quite sure that the image is completely dry before proceeding.

Above: A computer design printed straight onto encaustic card.

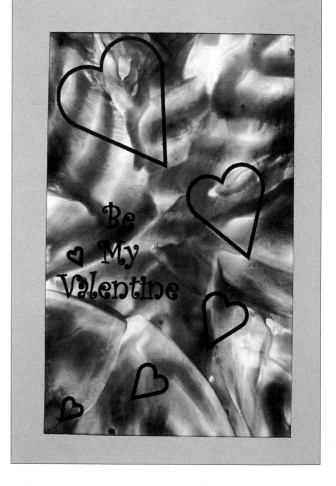

Above: Lots of clear wax with a hint of burgundy smoothed over with some lifting and dabbing.

Basic technique

First apply the image etc. to the encaustic card, using your chosen media.

The next step is to melt loads of clear wax onto the iron, and then add a small amount of coloured wax: it's best not to use the more opaque pastel shades or white. Now use the basic smoothing technique to cover the card. If the image looks too thickly covered with wax you can always (carefully) scrape some off, using the scribing tool or something similar, or you can try loading the iron with some more clear wax and smoothing over the picture again.

Above: Water effects always work well, as with these computer 'clip art' fish overlaid with clear wax and dabs of blue and green.

Sometimes we might want to build up more of a picture around our chosen silhouetted image. This can easily be done by using the basic iron manoeuvring techniques which we have already used in landscape painting, but making the picture more translucent by using clear wax mixed with the colours – especially over the silhouetted image itself.

Again, if the wax is a bit thick over the image you should carefully scrape some away. If you have a steady hand, it is possible to use a permanent marker pen over the top of the wax to make the image more prominent.

Blown-ink designs

With a brush or dropper, place a small pool of black ink directly on to the painting card. While the ink is still wet, use a drinking straw or the tube of an old biro pen in order to blow the ink in all directions.

A straw is all you need for this effect.

Experiment with how hard you blow, and try changing the angle of the straw in relation to the card. Experiment by holding the straw at different distances from the card – more ink can always be added. Let the whole thing dry, and then add the wax over the top. Finally, buff the whole thing up with tissue or a soft cloth.

SYMMETRICAL INK-BLOB PICTURES

Start with two identical-sized pieces of painting card.

Take the first card and carefully fold it in half. Open up the card and, on one side only, apply several blobs of ink.

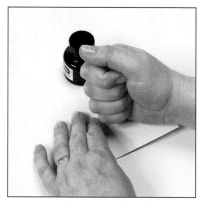

Re-fold the card and press firmly.

Quickly open up the folded card and, positioning it exactly over the second piece of card, again press down firmly and smooth it over with your hand. Carefully remove the folded card and – hey presto! – you should be left with a beautifully printed symmetrical pattern.

Once it is completely dry, carry on applying the wax over the top.

The second printing never comes out quite as strong as the first, but it still looks good. If you don't mind the fact that the first card has a fold down the middle, then you can use that as well.

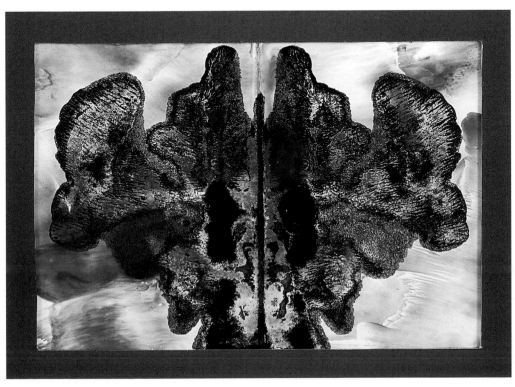

CALLIGRAPHY

I love the idea of using words to create pictures, although I have to say that I have found the use of a computer invaluable. Calligraphy in its basic form was, and is, done with pen and ink – but by more talented people than I. It is of course possible to trace words and phrases, transfer them onto the painting card and then go over them with ink.

Another variation on the same theme is to make a border with words, apply a translucent wax layer over the top of this and then paint a wax picture in the centre which corresponds to the words. Always remember to polish up your picture.

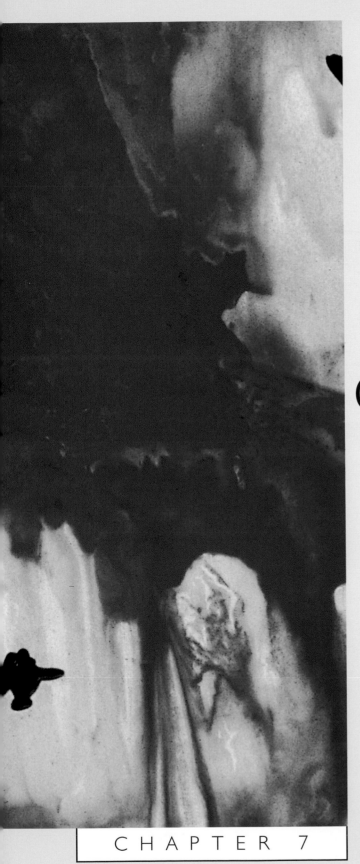

CREATING TEXTURES WITH WAX

In previous chapters we've looked at the basic techniques and the effects that can be achieved. In this section I want to show you some more ideas to use with your wax art. I discover these during 'play' sessions when I try out different things, seeing what works and what doesn't. I really would urge you to experiment: who knows what wonders you might unearth?

We can add texture to the wax by using such things as sand, salt, seed beads, seeds, wool, threads, raffia, feathers and tissue – the list could go on and on. This brings an extra dimension to what can be achieved.

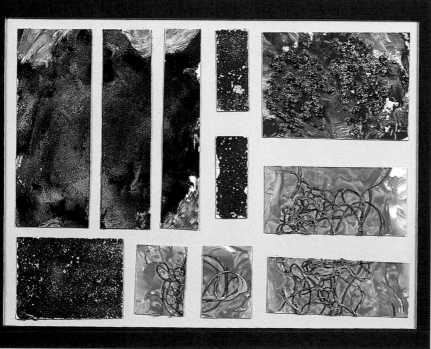

Above: This collage is made using several different textures.

This technique can be used in three main ways.

1. *To make abstract type pictures.*
2. *To be cut up and used in collages.*
3. *To add things such as sand, salt and seeds to landscape or fantasy pictures, or even to flower pictures – although this does take a delicate touch.*

Finding the right way to apply whatever texture you have chosen is often a matter of trial and error, with a little commonsense thrown in. You might think: 'What about adding some elastic bands to give texture to the wax? Wonderful – they could look like little worms wriggling around. But hold on just a minute: rubber or elastic bands would probably melt into a sticky mess as soon as the iron touched them . . .' Idea rejected!

The success with which each new texture can be mixed in with the wax will depend to some extent on whether you are trying to apply it to just a small section of a picture, which is tricky, or whether the end product is going to be left whole or cut up and used in some form of collage.

Left: Pastel colours and added sand give this picture a desert flavour.

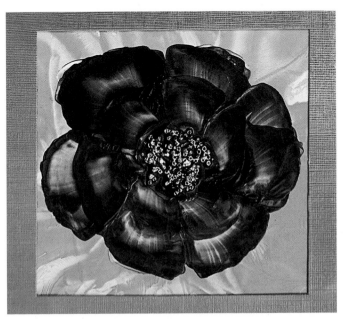

Right: This flower looks stunning with seed beads in the centre.

APPLYING TEXTURE TO A SMALL SECTION OF A PICTURE

There are two ways of doing this, both of which should begin with a new sheet of paper spread out on your work surface.

1. Sprinkle some fine silver sand, salt or other minuscule texturing medium onto a piece of paper. Place your finished picture, wax-side down on top of the sand or salt.

Gently place the iron on the back of the card for a few seconds, being very careful to heat only the part which you want textured (keep peeking under the card). For very small areas, use nothing but the very tip of the iron, and only very gently, on the back of the card - I did warn you that this was tricky! Use a soft paint brush or make-up brush to remove any loose particles: this also helps to polish up the textured wax as well.

2. Detach the iron's handle, lay the handle flat on the table, turn the iron upside down and slide the base plate into the handle so that it sits like a small hotplate.

It is now possible to melt the wax onto the iron hotplate. Work quickly, as the wax will rapidly cool down away from the heat and re-set.

To remove any set wax from your paint brush, simply place the brush head onto the hotplate, let the wax re-melt and then wipe quickly with a tissue. To get rid of all traces of coloured wax, melt a small amount of clear wax on to the hotplate, dip the brush head on to it and then again wipe with a tissue.

HOT TIP
Make sure that the part of the picture to which you want to add texture is thickly covered with wax.

HOT TIP
Make sure that your iron is unplugged and cooled down before dismantling it and turning it into a mini hotplate.

The iron can be secured by placing sticky tape along the edge.

Sprinkle some of your chosen texture medium (sand or salt, perhaps) into the melted wax.

Using a natural hair paint brush, pick up some of this textured wax from the hotplate and paint it onto the area on your picture where you want it.

Using the iron in its hotplate mode again, we can actually rest our painted wax picture on top of the iron so that it is heated from underneath. Once the wax on the picture is again in a molten state, a texture medium such as sand or salt can be carefully sprinkled onto the chosen area.

There are, however, some potential pitfalls. The texture medium, for example, can very easily be accidentally sprinkled on a part of the picture that you don't wish to be covered and, because it is very likely that the heated area will extend beyond the part you plan to be textured, the wax elsewhere may start to run and spoil the whole composition.

HOT TIP
Be extremely careful when putting sand or salt on to the hotplate of your iron, which can very easily become scratched.

APPLYING TEXTURE TO WAX TO BE USED IN COLLAGE

It's a much more straightforward process adding texture to wax when nothing else is going to appear on the painting card. We don't have to worry about the wrong areas of wax getting heated or texture medium travelling to places that it shouldn't.

It really is a lot of fun adding bits of thread and other random materials, and it also really gets your artistic juices going – well, it does mine!

Seed beads are brushed into place on the wax.

Threads are an interesting alternative medium.

Any texture medium can be introduced into the wax by using the iron in its hotplate mode. Place a plain piece of painting card on top of the hotplate and rub a coloured wax on to it: the wax will melt straight on to the card. Mix several colours if you like, and a touch of metallic colour (gold, silver, copper etc.) can be added, too.

The next step is to sprinkle or lay on the texture medium. Small granular-type mediums such as sand, salt, seed beads and seeds can be sprinkled on the melted wax and then moved around with a paint brush until all are covered and coated with wax and spread out as you wish. Salt and sand tend to soak up the wax so just sprinkling it on to the hot wax is often all you need to do. Carefully shake off the excess.

Other texture mediums like bits of thread, wool, raffia, feathers, dried grasses, sheep's wool, tissue, cotton wool and so on can be carefully placed in position on the melted wax, and then more melted wax can be applied with a paint brush over the top until the texture medium is coated and looking just how you want it.

HOT TIP
Mixing metallic wax colours into the ordinary coloured wax is particularly effective.

A final application of wax, and the work is finished.

Once the texture medium that you are using is in place then the card can be removed from the hotplate and allowed to cool. Your chosen texture medium (a feather, perhaps) should now be firmly stuck to the card by the wax. At this point you may choose to add extra colour to the top, so simply melt some wax onto the hotplate, pick it up with the paint brush and quickly apply it to the area you want.

The other way to combine the wax with a texture medium is to place your bits of material on a piece of painting card which has had a wax background of colour painted onto it, then load up the iron again with plenty of wax (either a single colour or any mixture you like) and smooth it over the top of the texture medium. Repeat this until you achieve a pleasing effect.

Left: Keep applying wax until all the wool strands are coated.

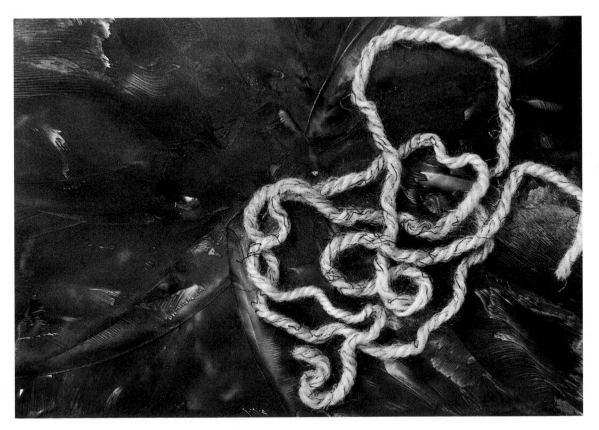

Above: Strands of wool look really good when waxed over.

PRINTING WITH WAX USING LEAVES AND FEATHERS

This is just like what the kids do at school with paint, but it's a bit more of a fiddle. Using leaves and feathers to print with wax can give some marvellous effects, especially after they have been polished up.

Collect a selection of leaves and feathers with different shapes, sizes and textures: this is very much a matter of trial and error. Place a leaf or feather (it doesn't matter which way up it is: experiment!) on a piece of the encaustic painting card, using it as a sort of pallet.

Load some wax onto your iron. With a feather it is best to smooth wax on to one side of the quill at a time, using the iron edge to get right in close to the side of the quill and then smoothing the iron outwards following the grain of the feather. Once both sides are covered with wax, smooth some along the quill itself.

When smoothing the wax over the leaves you may notice a slight smell of cooking vegetation. Don't worry about this, because even quite delicate little leaves are amazingly tough.

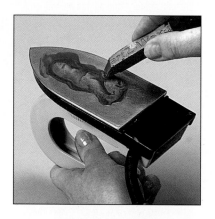

Using a plain colour with a metallic coloured wax mixed in on the iron gives a really nice effect.

Feathers take longer to cover with wax than leaves, and you may need to re-load your iron several times.

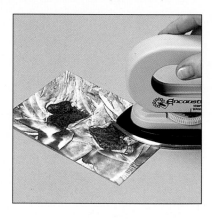

Leaves are very tough, and you'll find that you can re-use the same ones time after time.

Pulling the feather off can leave the card looking like a work of art in its own right.

Smoothing the iron over the feather may need to be repeated a couple of times to make sure that you get a good strong print.

It doesn't matter if the wax has cooled and set when removing the feather from the pallet card – just take hold of the tip of the quill and pull it off.

Leaves aren't quite robust enough to cope with this treatment, so they must be carefully lifted off of the pallet card when still warm. If the wax has cooled and the leaf has become stuck to the wax, simply smooth the iron over the top of it to re-heat it. If the leaf looks short of wax, just smooth on a bit more. The pallet cards can be used again and again when using that particular set of colours. It doesn't hurt to put the leaf or feather on top of wax which is already there.

Now place the leaf or feather wax-side down on a new piece of card and cover this with several layers of tissue.

When printing a feather, first hold the iron firmly on the tissue directly over the top of it: this will give you the imprint of the quill. Next smooth the iron first up one side of the quill, following the grain, and then up the other side. Uncover your print and pull the feather off it.

When printing a leaf or leaves hold the iron perfectly still, firmly pressing down on the tissue over the top of it. It is important not to move the iron about (as you would when ironing clothes)

because it tends to make the wax ooze out from the side of the leaf and spoil the image.

Once the printing is done you will probably find that the leaf has stuck to the painting card: use the blade of a craft knife to gently ease up the side and then carefully peel it off.

It is sometimes possible to obtain two prints from one printing if both sides have been covered with wax. This is achieved by inserting another piece of card on top of the leaf or feather and then covering this with tissue.

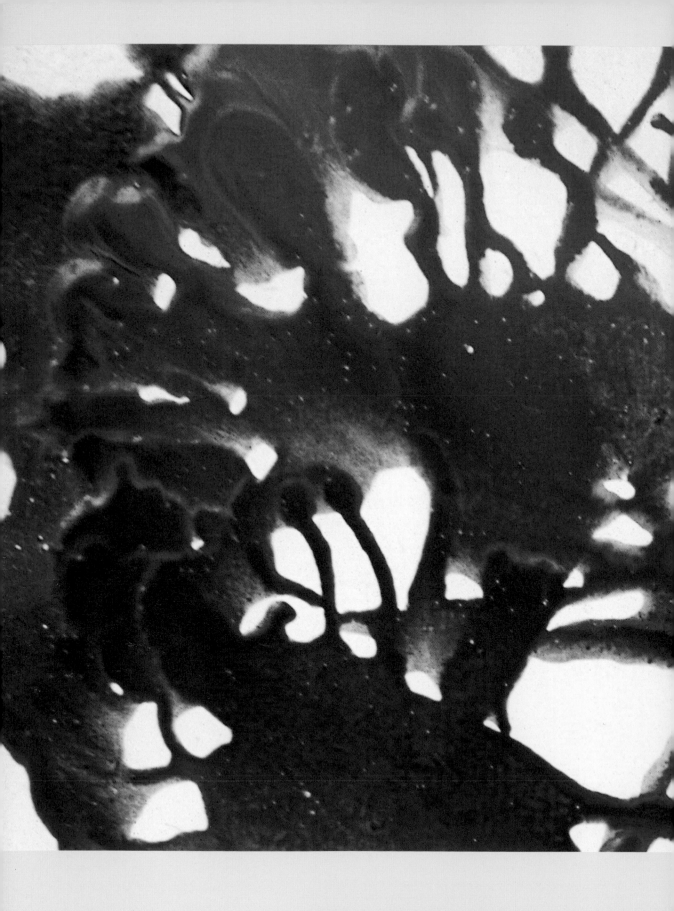

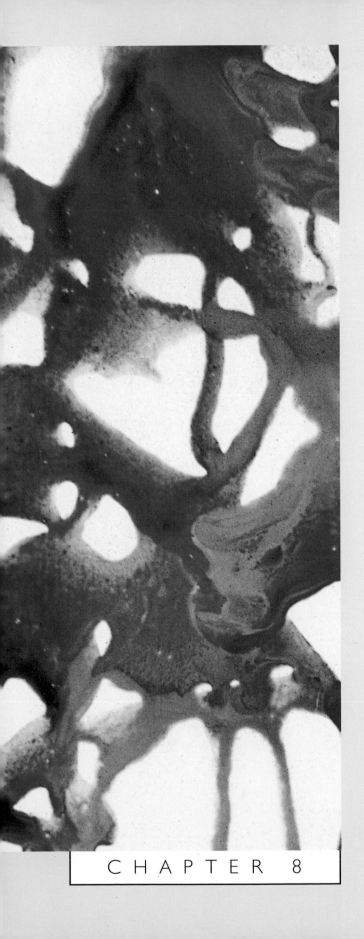

FRAMING YOUR PICTURES

Having spent time learning how to produce wondrous pieces of art, one of the great joys is having our hard work made into finished articles and displayed around us in our homes for all to enjoy. It's an equal pleasure being able to give pieces of our own work away to friends and family.

I have also managed to sell many of my wax art projects at craft fairs. If your ambition doesn't go quite as far as that, however, there are always lots of good causes trying to raise money, such as the local school fair, the Scouts and Guides and heaps of charities.

The most obvious and straightforward way to display your masterpieces is to frame them up as pictures to be hung on the wall or placed on the mantelpiece. There are a great many ready-made frames on offer in the shops. Often they will come with a mount card, and sometimes with a ready-made aperture, too. There are also plenty of shops that provide separate, ready-cut mount cards, and they can also be obtained via mail order.

The majority of the ready-cut mount cards available are cut with a bevelled or sloping edge, the idea being that it helps to draw the eye to the picture and stops any shadows being cast. The colour and texture range is vast: you may choose to pick a colour to match one in your wax picture or to have a completely contrasting one.

Although this is mainly a matter of personal taste, do

remember that the mount should complement the piece of art and that it needs to be more than just a coloured, narrow strip around the edge of the picture. It must work well with the frame, and you should take into account the place in which it is going to be displayed – you don't want it clashing with the wallpaper, after all.

You may like to have a go at cutting your own mount: sheets of mountboard can be obtained from most art and craft suppliers. You can either buy special bevel-edge mount-

cutters or cut the card and its aperture using a craft knife and a steel ruler – although in this case you will have to settle for the straight-cut option. Of course you don't have to use the thick type of mount card at all: ordinary coloured card can be used, or even paper. And what about using one of the wonderful range of hand made papers you can find these days?

There are many possibilities open to you, including the idea of using an abstract wax painting as a mount for a picture or photograph.

HOW TO CUT A MOUNT

The mount card must sit on the rebated ledge in the reverse side of the frame, so when taking the measurements do make sure that you take this into account.

Cross sections of frame, mount and picture.

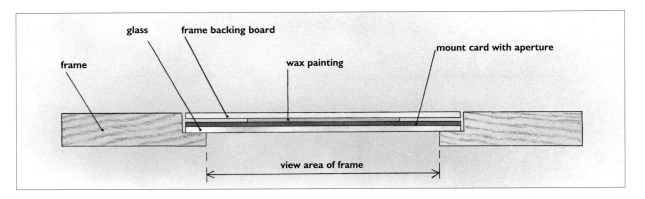

frame — *glass* — *frame backing board* — *wax painting* — *mount card with aperture* — *view area of frame*

Lay the mountboard on a cutting mat or a piece of board. Mark out the outer edges of the mount, checking carefully that everything is square before you cut.

Next mark out the window on the reverse side of the mountboard. The window needs to be slightly smaller all round than the picture you are mounting.

Measure in from the outer edges and again check that the corners are square – this is very important – and then, holding the knife at 90°, cut out the window. Stick double-sided tape on the reverse side of the mount, turn the mount over and place the picture on it. Finally, turn the mount and picture over onto the reverse side, and tape the picture edges in place using masking tape. This sticks the mount firmly onto the picture around the window opening so that the window doesn't gape.

OFF-CENTRE

If you want to get a really professional look when mounting your pictures, note that the visual centre of a framed picture is often not actually in the geographical centre. If the window is cut out exactly in the centre of the mount it can make the picture look top heavy, so to overcome this problem many pictures have a mount that is slightly deeper at the bottom than the top.

Use a sharp craft knife and a metal ruler to cut out the mount.

Make the cuts so that they only just meet in the corners.

HOT TIP

If you need to neaten any edges after cutting, especially in the corners, give them a very gentle sanding down, using the smoother side of an emery board.

Very sophisticated results can be achieved by adding thin parallel lines on the mount card around the aperture. The first should start no more than 5mm (³⁄₁₆in) from the window: a traditional pattern is two lines close together near the window, then a space of perhaps 20mm (³⁄₄in) and then another two lines close together. The lines can be made with a special ruling pen or, failing that, a very fine-tipped felt pen – gold and silver often look very effective.

On the reverse side of the mount, stick thin strips of double-sided tape about ¹⁄₃₂in (1mm) in from the edge of the window cut out.

Position your picture in front of you, remove the double sided tape backing and then, with the mount face up, carefully lower it into place on to the picture.

Right: Double mount cards will often enhance a picture.

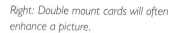

HOT TIP
Practise with your drawing pen first because some inks tend to bleed.

The other thing to remember, although I don't want to completely put you off, is that the slightest mistake is going to be glaringly obvious and could detract from your wax picture.

A striking way of mounting a picture is by taking a plain coloured straight-cut mount and applying to it either some cartridge paper or one of the many available hand-made papers. The inner and outer edges could be given a rough uncut look, either by tearing them or by using a pair of the special 'patterned edge' craft scissors which are now available.

If you have some reasonably long, trimmed-off pieces of wax-painted encaustic card which have been painted in an abstract design, you could carefully cut them down to a width of ½–³⁄₆₄in (1mm–2mm) and stick them onto the front of a mount either butting the corners or mitring them.

When framing up your art work always remember that you may want to give it some extra protection first, either by varnishing it with a quick-dry acrylic varnish or by covering it with clear sticky film.

Before you do either of these things, make sure that you give your wax picture a good buff up with a soft cloth or tissues. Please note that some varnishes take quite a lot longer to dry on wax than they do on other things.

PAINTING WOODEN FRAMES

To wax paint a wooden frame successfully you need to choose one which has a completely flat surface. Make sure that the wood is sealed before you start.

My husband made me these two frames from MDF, but you can buy very similar frames in the shops and by mail order. Both were sealed with two coats of acrylic paint: the purple design used hot air and the green frame was decorated with the encaustic iron by lifting and dabbing.

I bought this little wooden box frame and painted it with dark blue and gold coloured wax using the lifting and dabbing method. I then sprayed a few shells and a piece of drift wood with gold paint and stuck them onto the backing board.

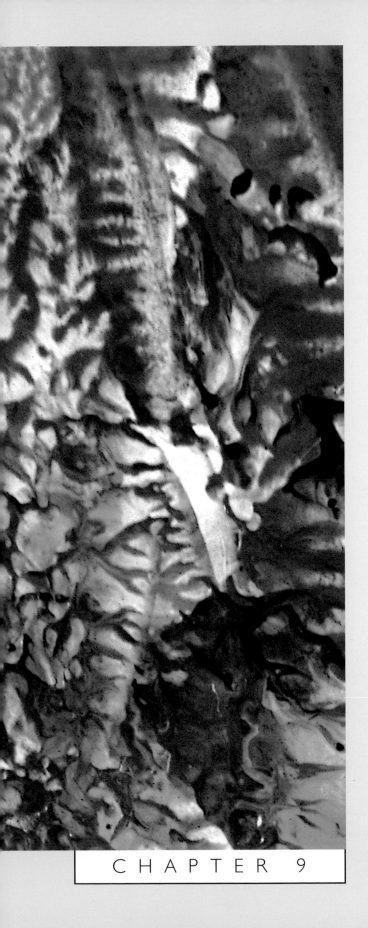

Wax Printing on Fabric

This sounds a bit scary, doesn't it? In fact it is fairly straightforward and can give some very rewarding results, especially if you like needlework and embroidery. The technique works best on fabrics such as cotton, linen and silk which, being natural, are more absorbent than man-made ones. White or light-coloured fabric should be used, since not much of the wax transfer would show up on dark material, and it is also advisable to use fabric which has a fairly close weave: more open weaves tend to make the print rather indistinct.

Try to ensure that your original wax picture or pattern has a reasonably even amount of wax on, it with no blobby bits and no sparse areas. It is also important to get the iron at just the right temperature when actually transferring the wax print to fabric, so always practise first on scraps before you let yourself loose on that new white T-shirt bought especially for the purpose.

BASIC TECHNIQUE

First of all prepare your wax picture or pattern. You can do this on the normal wax painting card (diagram 1), but I often use the larger sized white ceramic wall tiles (diagram 2). These can be cleaned and used again very easily by just smoothing the iron over to heat them (they retain the heat longer than card) and then wiping them with tissue.

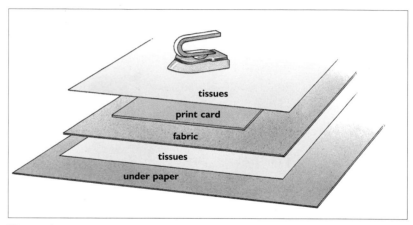

Diagram 1

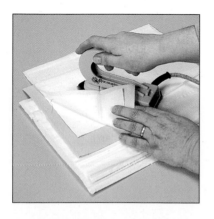

You must iron on top of the tissue over the back of the fabric which is being pressed on to the tile.

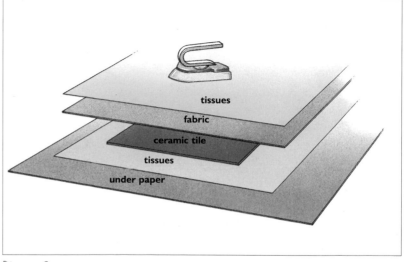

Diagram 2

Place clean under-paper on your work surface; cover it with two or three layers of tissues; and then position your chosen fabric on top. If you are printing on a T-shirt or anything which is not a single thickness of fabric you will need to arrange the fabric item so that only one layer is on top of the paper and tissue.

With a T-shirt, just place the paper and tissue inside it between the two layers of material. Make sure the fabric has no creases or puckers on the area that is to be printed. Next carefully position the wax-painted card, wax-side down, on the fabric, cover the back of the wax card with tissue (to protect the fabric from dirt) and then iron over the back of the card – making sure that the heat setting is just above low.

If using ceramic wall tiles to print from, then the fabric and wall tile should be in reverse positions to that of the fabric and painting card.
In most cases the fabric will now need to be washed to remove the wax and leave just the coloured pigment. This is done by giving the printed fabric a short, hot handwash. After this, for clothes and home furnishings etc., only ever handwash in warm water, preferably with a non-biological washing powder.

There are certain instances when you may not want to wash the wax out of the fabric – for example when the print is going to be used as the background for a piece of embroidery. The problem that you may encounter here is that the wax could very easily mark the embroidery threads, especially the lighter colours.

Furthermore, warm hands handling fabric which has wax on it could spell disaster, with dirty marks getting everywhere. The way to overcome these problems is to make sure that the whole of the printed wax picture is encased within an embroidery frame or hoop, and that when you are stitching on the picture you are very, very careful not to touch the fabric too much. I would suggest that the safest thing to do is to wash out the wax before doing any embroidery so that you are left with only the pigment image: this also means that the piece of embroidery can be washed again (if necessary) before it is framed.

Any type of wax painting can be transferred onto fabric, whether it a landscape, fantasy picture, a floral picture or an abstract. Landscapes are particularly good for embroidery and would look equally good as either a framed picture or on the front of a T-shirt.

Left: Wax can be applied directly to feathers and leaves and then printed onto the fabric.

Below: Abstract designs can look stunning when printed onto cushion covers, bags and T-shirts.

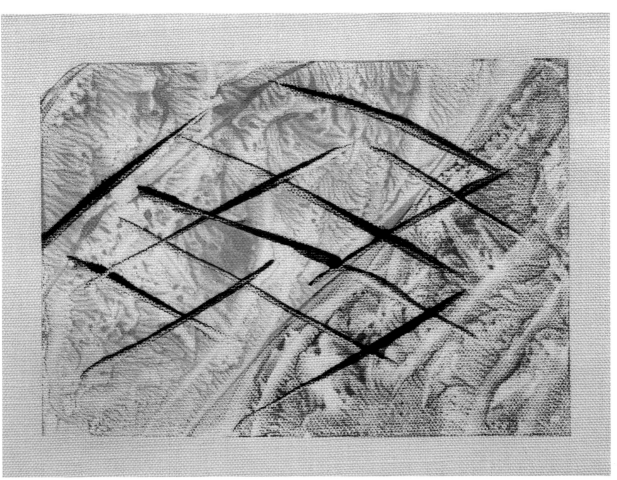

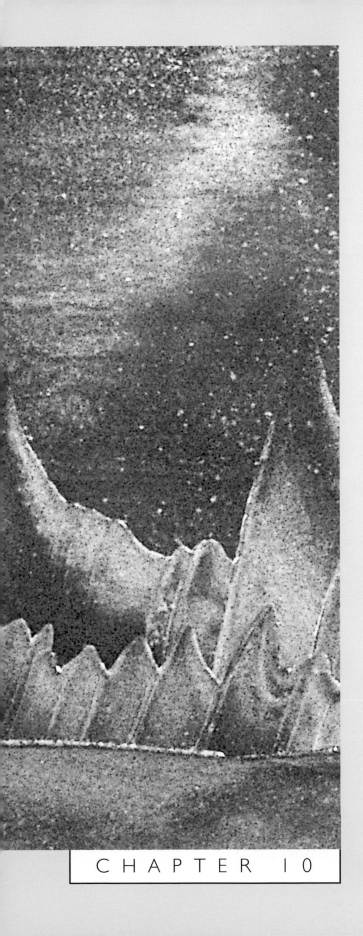

PROJECTS USING
WAX ART

CHAPTER 10

GREETINGS CARDS, BOOKMARKS AND GIFT TAGS

Blanks for these are readily available in art and craft shops, and there are some really good mail order suppliers, usually offering very reasonable prices. The available choice is almost breathtaking, with every imaginable colour, a vast number of sizes and shapes, textures galore and every shape of window – some with printed borders and some with printed greetings.

It is vitally important to protect the wax surfaces of things which are going to be handled a lot and which might be damaged in the post. As with framed pictures, polish the wax art first and then varnish with an acrylic varnish, using either a brush or a spray can. The alternative is to cover with clear self adhesive film.

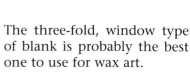

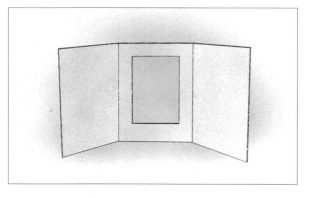

The three-fold, window type of blank is probably the best one to use for wax art.

The simplest and least expensive way of making a greetings card from your wax art is to stick the wax painting straight on to the front of a bi-fold card, leaving a small border of card showing around the edge.

If you take this option, it is important that you make sure the edges of the wax painting are neat, since the wax on the outer edges of a painting often tends to be rather thick and messy looking. This is easily solved by trimming the edges back with a craft knife or a pair of patterned edge craft scissors.

Left: Bi-fold card with wax art stuck directly on the front, trimmed with craft scissors.

Right: You can cut your own greeting card blanks from coloured card.

Card ideas

Wax paint an A6-sized piece of encaustic card with an abstract design. Cut out a 1in (2.5cm) square window in the middle and back it with a piece of coloured card that complements the design. Now paint or draw a very simple picture to represent the occasion the card is for (a gold heart for Valentine's Day, a line-drawn Christmas tree), or write a greeting.

Right: Mounted abstract wax art with window and heart.

One of the lovely things about making your own greetings cards is that you are able to personalize them and make them suit the person they will be sent to. When making a pretty floral card it's really nice to be able to add a bow or something similar. Another advantage is that you can make the card to fit absolutely any occasion – some of which, after all, aren't generally well covered by the commercial card companies.

Don't forget that wax art can be used to make great gift tags as well – they are just scaled-down greetings cards. Another striking idea for a gift tag is to wax print a leaf, then carefully cut out the shape and use this as a tag.

Bookmark ideas

I think it's lovely to give a bookmark as a little gift because, although they are often no more expensive than a card, they have a much longer life and are something which will be used. Again there are many blank bookmark mounts available (mail order and in the shops) but, as with greetings cards, you can easily make your own. Adding a tassel can look really good.

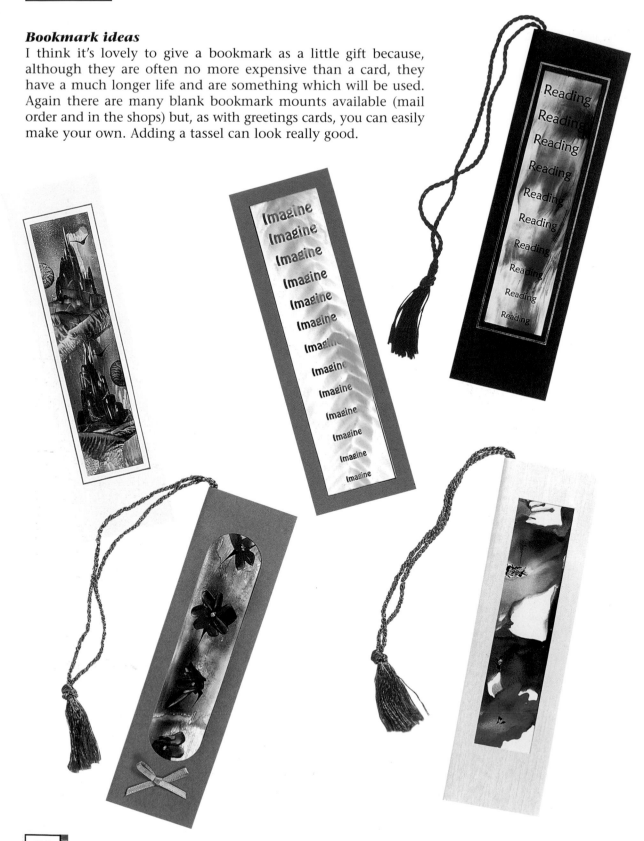

CALENDARS

It's possible to buy calendar kits, which usually contain a double-fold mount, a calendar pad and a self-adhesive hook – you only have to create a wonderful piece of wax art and put it all together.

Calendar

Calendar

Calendar

A calendar is basically a mounted picture with a calendar pad hanging at the bottom. As with mounting pictures, you can either affix it to the back of a window mount or simply trim the edges of your wax painting and attach it directly to a larger piece of card. Again, the mounts can be embellished with fine lines, hand-made papers and so on, and double mounts can also be used – the choice is yours.

CLEAR FOLDER

This is a very quick and easy vehicle for your wax art. I picked up this clear folder in my local stationers – it could be used for school work, recipes, knitting patterns, photographs or a whole host of other things. Simply mount your painting on the inside of the front cover, using self adhesive film.

BOXES

These days there is an abundance of different ready-made boxes available to buy in craft shops and by mail order – wooden, papier maché and cardboard. Remember that if the boxes have not been sealed and are in their raw state they tend to be too porous to take wax directly when you need to move it around. This can be easily remedied by applying several coats of varnish first, by priming the surface to be painted with acrylic paint or by sealing it with a watered down solution of PVA glue.

WAX PAINTED CLOCK

I have to say that I was very pleased with the end results of this. Clock workings can be bought, and the battery type is usually quite reasonably priced. I happened to have an old clock which I took apart.

Start with an off-cut of ¼in (6mm) MDF or plywood (this one is MDF). Don't try to use anything much thicker, because the clock spindle won't fit. Draw round a dinner plate to mark out a circle and cut it out, using a fret saw – or get someone to do it for you. (Thanks, Steve!) You will also need to drill a hole in the centre the right size to take the part of the clock workings to which you fix the hands.

Always wear a dust mask when cutting and drilling wood, especially MDF. I used a design created by blowing hot air, which I happen to think lends itself particularly well to this type of project.

Buff the wax finish up to a lovely shine and protect it by giving it at least two coats of varnish. Complete the project by assembling the clock parts. My clock has a face, but some workings are supplied with stick-on numbers.

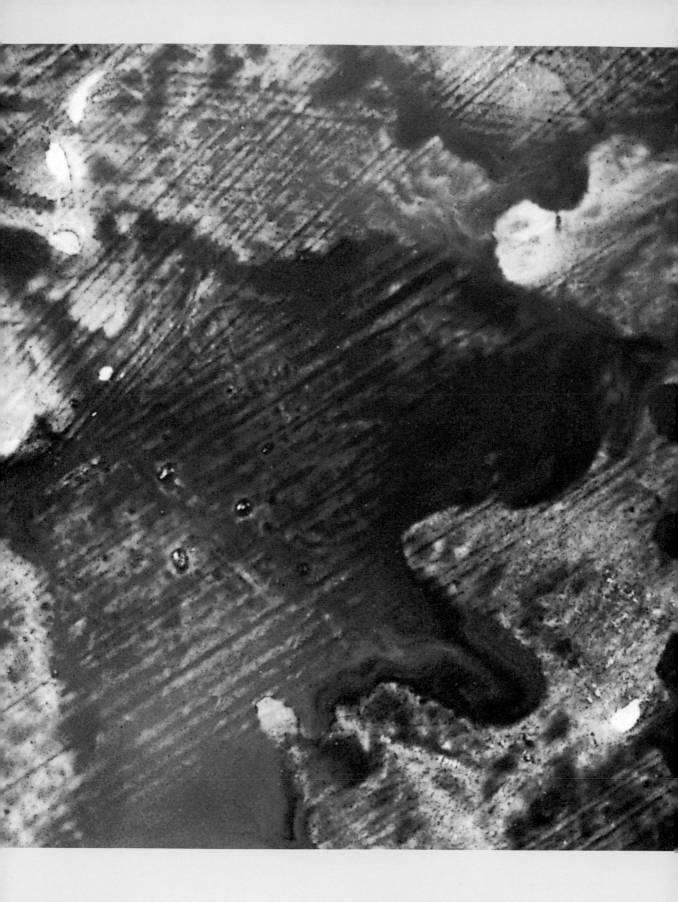

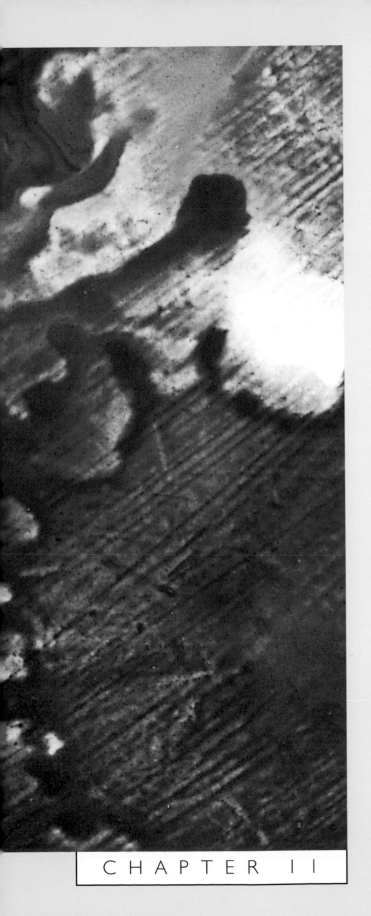

Projects Using Wax Printing on Fabric

T-SHIRTS

Don't forget when printing onto a T-shirt or anything which is not a single thickness of fabric that you will need to arrange it so that only one layer is on top of the paper and tissue. With a T-shirt just place the paper and tissue inside it between the two layers of material. You can print any wax art on a T-shirt – fantasy, floral, landscape or abstract – but I think these two examples are great fun.

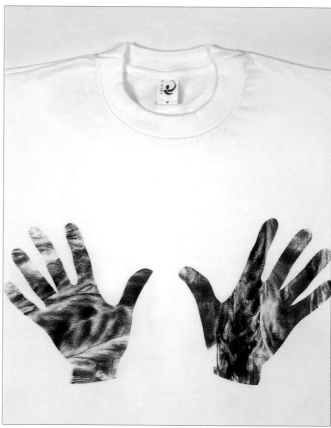

The hearts were drawn free-hand on the reverse side of a piece of encaustic painting card. (It doesn't matter if they are a bit off-centre – it adds to the appeal.) Turn the card over and wax paint in bright red any abstract design you like: mine was done using the lifting and dabbing method. Then simply cut out the heart shapes, arrange them face down on the front of the T-shirt, cover with several layers of tissue and print them by ironing. Finish as usual by giving it a hot handwash to get rid of the wax. The hands were done in the same way, by drawing round my hands on the back of the card and then painting an abstract design using red and blue.

TOTE BAGS

I love these seaside theme tote bags, and they are very quick and easy to make. I particularly like the idea of using knotted cord as loops for the draw-string to go through.

Materials:
Cotton fabric 17½ x 27½in (45 x 70cm)
6½ft (2m) of thick white piping cord
White thread.

Cut the fabric in half so that you have two pieces 45cm x 35cm (17½ x 13¾in).
　Now take a piece of encaustic painting card, and either draw a very basic stylised boat on to the back of it or trace the template provided.

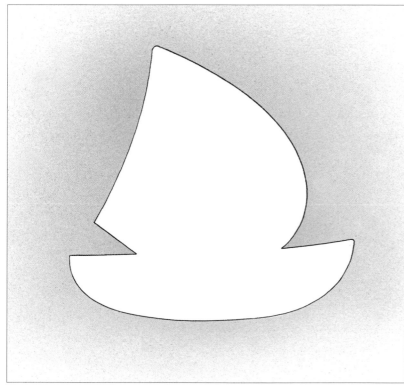

Wax paint an abstract design in blue on the front: Wriggle the iron to give an impression of waves. Turn the card over and carefully cut out the boat shape, using a craft knife, then trim the outer edges of the card to neaten them or use patterned craft scissors to cut round the outer edges.
　Print this on the front of one piece of the fabric following the instructions in the fabric printing chapter. Position the wax card on the fabric, centring it from side to side and placing the bottom of the card approximately 4in (10cm) up from the bottom.
　Hot handwash to remove wax. I back-stitched round the boat shape in white thread to make it stand out a bit more.

To make the knotted cord loops for the draw string simply tie a single granny knot in the end of the cord; leave a gap of about ¾in (2cm) and tie another one; pull the knots really tight; and then cut the cord roughly ⅜in (1cm) from the knots. Repeat this until you have six loops.

The next thing to do is to mark out on your fabric pieces where the knotted cord loops go (the back is the same as the front but without the wax print). Sew them on by hand.

Put the front and back fabric panels' right sides together and then pin, baste and machine- or hand-stitch the two sides and bottom of the bag ⅝in (1.5cm) in from the edge. Trim the seam allowances and turn the bag the right way out. Double-fold in the raw top edge of the bag, press and sew.

To complete the bag, thread a length of cord through the knotted cord loops and then tie the two ends together with a reef knot.

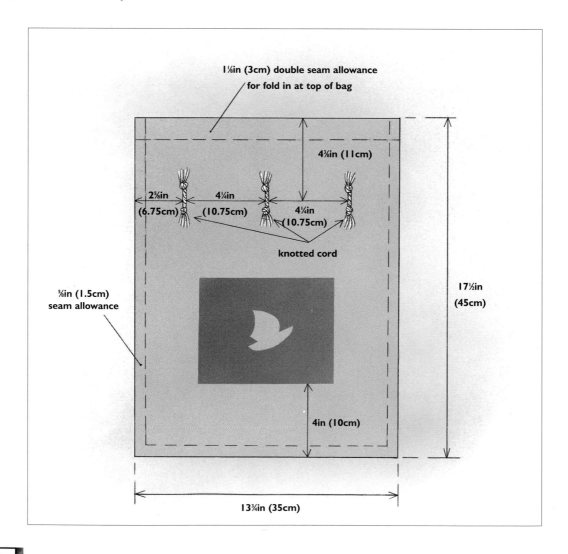

Small tote bag

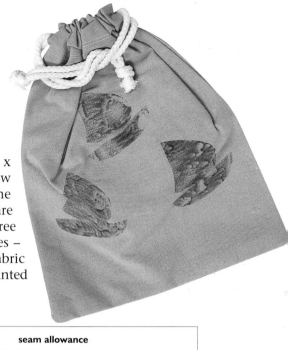

Materials:
Cotton fabric 20 x 13¾in (50cm x 35cm)
3ft 3in (1 metre) thick piping cord
White thread

Cut the fabric so you have two pieces 13¾ x 10in (35cm x 25cm). Next take some encaustic painting card and draw three boats on the reverse side. Wax paint the front of the card in an abstract style and cut out the boat shapes. Prepare the front panel of fabric for printing, and arrange the three boat shapes on the right side of the fabric at jaunty angles – try to centre the boat arrangement on the section of fabric which will show once the bag is made up. Once you have printed the boats, give the fabric a hot hand-wash and dry.

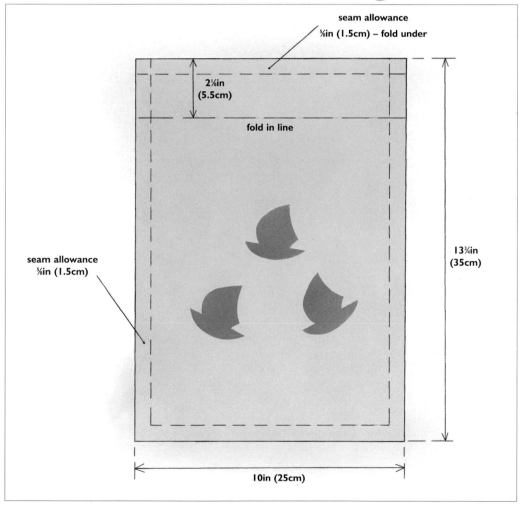

seam allowance
⅝in (1.5cm) – fold under

2⅛in (5.5cm)

fold in line

seam allowance ⅝in (1.5cm)

13¾in (35cm)

10in (25cm)

Make the bag up by placing the front and back panels' right sides together; pin, baste and stitch up the three seams leaving the top open; and trim the seam allowances. Turn the bag the right way out. At the top of the bag fold under the ⅝in (1.5cm) seam allowance and press. Fold in another 1⅝in (4cm), press again and then stitch round 1⅜in (3.5cm) down from the top – a double row of stitching about ¾₂in (1mm) apart can look very nice.

Unpick about ⅝in (1.5cm) of both side seams in the middle of the draw-cord tube. Stitch to fasten the ends where the seam has been unpicked. Cut the piping cord in half and thread one piece through so that both ends come out on one side on the bag, tie the two ends together with a reef knot and then thread the other piece of piping cord through so that both ends come out on the opposite side of the bag. Tie the two ends together with a reef knot. If you hold the two sets of cords on either side of the bag and pull you will now find that the bag will gather up at the top and close beautifully.

BACK PACK

Materials:
Cotton fabric 27½ x 17¾in (70 x 45cms)
Circle of fabric 8in (20cm) diameter
9ft 9in (3m) cord
Thread

Cut the fabric so that you have two pieces 13¾ x 10in (35cm x 25cm) plus a circle with a diameter of 8in (20cm). Take some encaustic painting card, and wax paint whatever picture you like – I've done one back pack with hot air-blown flowers and one with an abstract design. Print your wax painting on to the front panel of the fabric, and then give the fabric a hot handwash and dry.

Make the back pack up by placing the front and back panels right sides together; pin, baste and stitch up the two side seams, leaving the top and bottom open; and trim the seam allowances. Pin the circle of fabric right sides together into the bottom of the bag tube, and then baste and stitch.

Turn the bag the right way out. At the top of the bag, fold under the ⅝in (1.5cm) seam allowance and press. Fold in another 1⅝in (4cm), press again and then stitch round 1⅜in (3.5cm) down from the top. Unpick about ⅝in (1.5cm) of both side seams in the middle of the draw cord tube at the top of the bag. Stitch to fasten the ends where the seam has been undone. Cut the cord in half, and thread one piece through so that both ends come out on one side of the bag. Thread the other piece of cord through so that both ends come out on the opposite side of the bag, and pull the two sets of cords to close the top.

Sew two `D' rings onto the bottom of the back pack – one where each side seam meets the circle base. Thread one set of cords through each `D' ring, adjust the length of the cords so that the back pack sits on your back comfortably and knot the cords onto the `D' rings.

CUSHIONS

There are many different ways to close a cushion cover – zips, ties, flap-overs, pillow slip-type inside flap, buttons and so on – and it's just a matter of choosing which style of closer you wish to use.

The average cushion cover panel size is around 18in (46cm): add seam allowances to this and you will need two pieces of fabric approximately 19¼in (49cm) square.

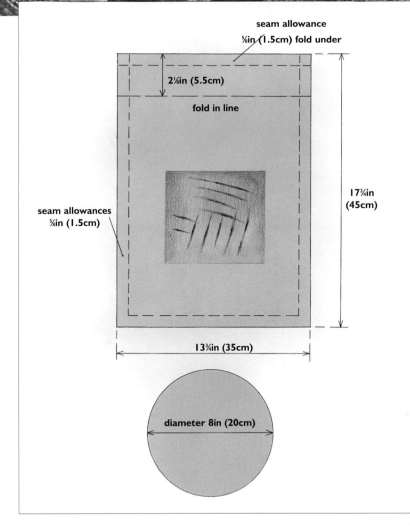

seam allowance
⅝in (1.5cm) fold under

2⅛in (5.5cm)

fold in line

seam allowances
⅝in (1.5cm)

17¾in (45cm)

13¾in (35cm)

diameter 8in (20cm)

I have edged my cushion cover with a contrasting strip, picking out the two main colours in the wax art prints. I reduced the printed fabric size to accommodate the extra edging. To achieve this very modern effect I wax painted four ceramic tiles with an abstract design, making two sets of two tiles that looked similar. After printing, washing and drying I sewed the cushion cover together and used ribbon ties to keep the cover closed. It must be a hit, because as soon as it was finished my teenage daughter asked if she could have it for her bedroom.

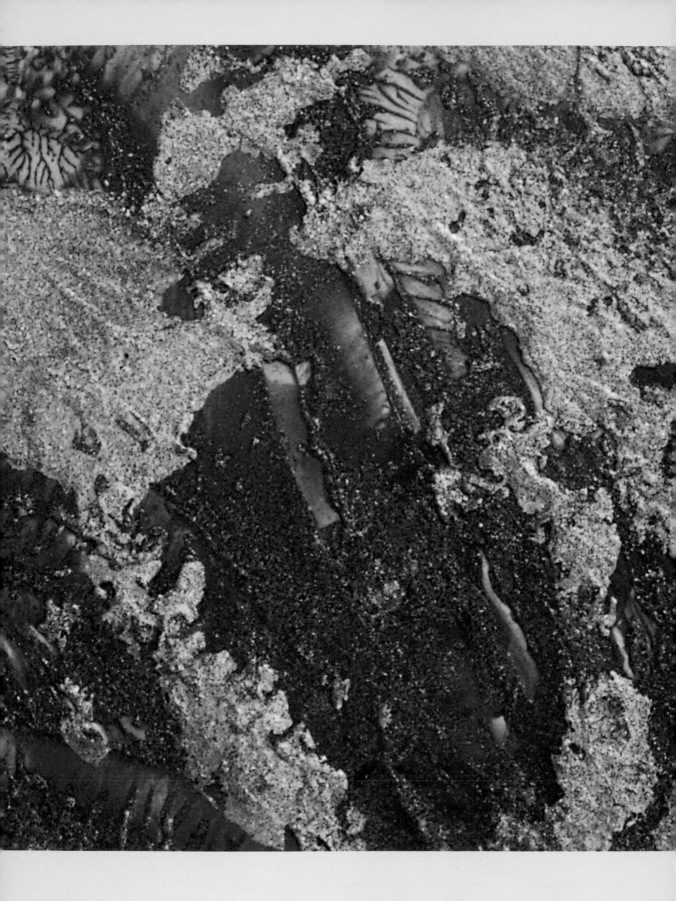

GALLERY

CHAPTER 12

Picture: 'cut up water'

Card: indirect wax transfer design

Pine frame with four windows and blown wax flowers

Lilac parcel with matching
card and gift tag

Card: congratulations

Card: airbrush design

Card: Easter

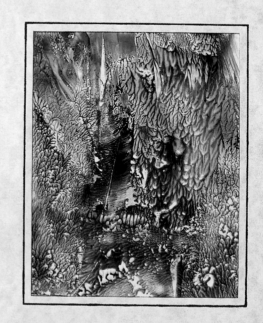

Best Wishes

Card: abstract

Card: Good luck

Card: Christmas holly

Card: printed ivy leaf

Happy Christmas

Christmas card with star

Christmas gift tag

Gift tag: Christmas holly

Card: Christmas candles

Gift tag: purple abstract

Card: airbrush heart design

Small mounted picture: blown wax design

Gift tag: fantasy

Small mounted picture: blown wax design

Small mounted picture: blown wax design

Small mounted picture: blown wax design

Small mounted picture: blown wax design

Card: butterflies

Mounted embroidery

Card: Northern Lights abstract

Card: printed gold leaves

ACKNOWLEDGEMENTS

I would like to thank the following for their generous help with art and craft supplies, materials and tools:

Michael Bossom of Arts Encaustic International for his friendliness, help, advice and encouragement.

Arts Encaustic International.
Glogue, Dyfed, Wales, UK., SA36 0ED
Tel: (01239) 831401 Fax: 831767
E-mail:info@encaustic.com
Website: www.encaustic.com
Mail Order Encaustic art materials and equipment.

Art Van Go.
16 Hollybush Lane, Datchworth, Knebworth, Herts, SG3 6RE
Tel: (01438) 814946 Fax: 816267
E-mail artvango@talk21.com
Mobile shop and mail order arts and crafts supplies including handmade papers.
On-line shopping on its way.

Axminster Power Tool Centre / Tools and Machinery.
Chard Street, Axminster, Devon.
Telesales: 0800 371822 Technical Sales & Enquiries: 01297 33656
Customer Service: 0345 585290
Fax: 01297 35242
E-mail: email@axminster.co.uk
Website: www.axminster.co.uk
Shops, on-line shopping and mail order catalogue.

Coats Crafts UK.
Lingfield, McMullen Road, Darlington, County Durham, DL1 1GA.
For enquiries and stockists
                Tel: +44 (0) 1325 394237
E-mail: consumer.ccuk@coats.com
Website: www.coatscrafts.co.uk
Embroidery Materials and threads etc.

Craft Creations Ltd., - Greeting card blanks and accessories
 Ingersoll House, Delamare Road, Cheshunt, Hertfordshire, EN8 9HD.
Tel: (01992) 781900 Fax: 634339
E-mail: enquiries@craftcreations.com
Website: http://www.craftcreations.com
Shop, on line shopping and mail order catalogue. Greeting card blanks and accessories, craft supplies including paper, card, die cut mounts, transfers, calendar pads and kits and much more.

Craft Depot.
Somerton Business Park, Somerton, Somerset, TA11 6SB.
Tel: 01458 27 47 27 Fax: 01458 27 29 32
E-mail craftdepot@aol.com Website: www.craftdepot.co.uk
On line shopping and craft supplies catalogue

Homecrafts Direct.
PO Box 38, Leicester, LE1 9BU.
Tel: 0845 458 4531. Fax: 458 4793.
E-mail: info @homecrafts.co.uk
Website: www.homecrafts.co.uk
On line shopping and mail order arts and crafts catalogue.

Panduro Hobby.
Orders: Freepost Transport Avenue, Brentford, Middlesex, TW8 8BR.
Tel orders: 01392 427788 Customer Services: (020) 8847 6161
Fax: (020) 8847 5073
E-mail: pandurohobby@compuserve.com
Website: www.pandurohobby.whd.net
On line shopping and mail order catalogue art craft supplies.

Skil power tools.
PO Box 98, Broad Water Park, Denham, Uxbridge, Middlesex, UB9 5HJ
Power tools including hot air paint strippers.

Winsor & Newton, ColArt Fine Arts & Graphics Ltd.,
Whitefriars Avenue, Harrow, Middlesex, HA3 5RH, England.
Tel: 020 8427 4343 Fax 020 8863 7177
Website: www.winsornewton.com
Artists' materials including paints, paint mediums, inks, brushes, paper etc.

ABOUT THE AUTHOR

In 1997 Hazel Marsh moved to Cornwall from Kent with her husband, teenage son and daughter, following a lifelong dream to live near the sea in the English West Country. Part of that dream was to live more creatively, and after trying her hand at many different arts and crafts she made the happy discovery of wax art. Hazel has exhibited and demonstrated her work at craft fairs and hopes to write more books on other craft subjects.

INDEX

A SELECTION OF CRAFT TITLES AVAILABLE FROM
GMC Publications